和月伸宏

NOBUHIRO WATSUKI

WATSUKI IS A LIAR.

AS YOU MAY HAVE FIGURED FROM THE ABOVE COMMENTS, I'VE REALLY GOT A THING FOR KENSHIN'S ENEMIES, THE SHINSENGUMI. GIVEN THAT I'M HISTORY-ILLITERATE AND DIDN'T EVEN TAKE JAPANESE HISTORY IN HIGH SCHOOL, I GUESS THAT MAKES ME AN IMPOSTER, HUH?

EVEN SO, THE BOOK YOU'RE NOW HOLDING IS NOT ONLY MY FIRST COLLECTED VOLUME, BUT MY DEBUT WORK. IDIOT CHILD OF MINE THOUGH IT MAY BE, PLEASE TRY AND LOVE IT, NONETHELESS.

Rurouni Kenshin, which has found fans not only in Japan but around the world, first made its appearance in 1992, as an original short story in Japan's **Weekly Shonen Jump Special**. Later rewritten and published as a regular, continuing **Jump** series in 1994, **Rurouni Kenshin** ended serialization in 1999 but continued in popularity, as evidenced by the 2000 publication of **Yahiko no Sakabatô** ("Yahiko's Reversed-Edge Sword") in Japan's **Weekly Shonen Jump**. His most current work, **Busô Renkin** ("Armored Alchemist"), began publication this June, also in Japan's **Jump**.

RUROUNI KENSHIN VOL. 1
The SHONEN JUMP Graphic Novel Edition

STORY AND ART BY
NOBUHIRO WATSUKI

English Adaptation/Gerard Jones
Translation/Kenichiro Yagi
Touch-Up Art & Lettering/Steve Dutro
Cover, Graphics & Layout Design/Sean Lee
Editor/Avery Gotoh

Supervising Editor/William Flanagan/Kit Fox
Managing Editor/Elizabeth Kawasaki
Director of Production/Noboru Watanabe
Executive V.P./Editor-in-Chief/Hyoe Narita
Sr. Director of Licensing and Acquisitions/Rika Inouye
V.P. of Sales & Marketing/Liza Coppola
V.P. of Strategic Development/Yumi Hoashi
Publisher/Seiji Horibuchi

PARENTAL ADVISORY
Rurouni Kenshin may contain violence, language and alcohol or tobacco usage.
It is rated "T+" for older teens.

RUROUNI KENSHIN ©1994 by NOBUHIRO WATSUKI. All rights reserved. First published in Japan in 1994 by SHUEISHA Inc., Tokyo. English translation rights in the United States of America and Canada arranged by SHUEISHA Inc. The stories, characters, and incidents mentioned in this publication are entirely fictional. No portion of this book may be reproduced or transmitted in any form or by any means without written permission from the copyright holders.

Printed in Canada.

Published by VIZ, LLC
P.O. Box 77010 • San Francisco, CA 94107

SHONEN JUMP Graphic Novel Edition
10 9 8 7 6 5
First printing, October 2003
Second printing, November 2003
Third printing, February 2004
Fourth printing, July 2004
Fifth printing, September 2004

www.viz.com

THE WORLD'S MOST POPULAR MANGA
SHONEN JUMP GRAPHIC NOVEL
www.shonenjump.com

SHONEN JUMP GRAPHIC NOVEL

Rurouni Kenshin™

Vol. 1

MEIJI SWORDSMAN ROMANTIC STORY

STORY AND ART BY

NOBUHIRO WATSUKI

CONTENTS

Rurouni Kenshin
Meiji Swordsman Romantic Story
Volume One

Act 1
Kenshin • Himura Battōsai
5

Act 2
Rurouni in the City
57

Act 3
Tokyo Samurai
81

Act 4
Kasshin-Ryū Reborn
104

Act 5
The Fight Merchant
125

Act 6
Face Off: Sagara Sanosuke
145

END-OF-VOLUME SPECIAL
RUROUNI
MEIJI SWORDSMAN ROMANTIC STORY
169

Act 1 — Kenshin • Himura Battōsai

140 YEARS AGO IN KYOTO, WITH THE COMING OF THE "BLACK SHIPS"...
...THERE AROSE A WARRIOR CALLED HITOKIRI BATTŌSAI.
FELLING MEN WITH HIS BLOOD-STAINED BLADE, HE CLOSED THE TURBULENT BAKUMATSU ERA...
...AND SLASHED OPEN THE AGE KNOWN AS MEIJI.
THEN HE VANISHED, AND WITH THE FLOW OF YEARS, BECAME A LEGEND.
IN THE 11TH YEAR OF MEIJI, IN THE MIDDLE OF TOKYO...
...THIS TALE BEGINS...

Act 1

Kenshin • Himura Battōsai

HITOKIRI BATTŌSAI !!
I'VE FOUND YOU.
HSSSS
FOR TWO MONTHS YOU HAVE MURDERED AT WILL!
NOW IT ENDS!
ORO?

READ THIS WAY

DON'T PLAY THE FOOL!
WHO ELSE WOULD DEFY THE LAW AND CARRY A SWORD IN THIS NIGHT?!
HO.
!!
NK!
TRAK
...THIS... IS THE HITOKIRI BATTŌSAI?
NOPE.

*A SWORD WITH THE BLADE UPSIDE DOWN.

THEN... YOU'RE REALLY JUST...
A RUROUNI, YES. ♡
BUT WHY CARRY A BLADE YOU CAN'T USE?
PWIIiiiii
!
POLICE WHISTLE!
I HAVE TO GO...!!
TOSS
ORO!
IT SEEMS...
...THERE'S SOMETHING INTERESTING TO CHECK OUT HERE.
YAAAA
SSSHHHH

DMMMMMM
WEAK WEAK WEAK!!
WEAK!!
YOU ARE ALL TOO WEAK!
SO... STRONG ...
...HE MUST BE...
...THE LEGENDARY BATTŌSAI !!
VSH

THIS IS IT, BATTŌSAI !!
PTT
!!
ZZZZZZZZZZ
THK
OH.

!
UHH...
!!
YOU'RE QUITE THE RISK-TAKER.
RURO--

READ THIS WAY

RUNNING WHILE WOUNDED CAN BE DEADLY.
NOW THAT HE'S TOLD US HIS SWORD-FIGHTING STYLE WE DON'T HAVE TO BE SO--
KAMIYA KASSHIN-RYŪ IS MY STYLE!!
HE MURDERS IN OUR NAME!!
VSH
I'M GOING TO--
REMEMBER. NO RUNNING.
TNG
JERK
RK
YOU WON'T CATCH HIM ANY-WAY.
LET'S LEAVE BEFORE THE POLICE DECIDE TO QUESTION US.
KAMIYA KASSHIN-RYŪ KENJUSTU (SWORD ARTS) DOJO
神谷活心流
剣術道場

"KAMIYA KASSHIN-RYŪ."
"KAMIYA KAORU--"
"--INSTRUCTOR."
ORO?
WE WERE A SMALL DOJO.
BUT WE HAD TEN GOOD STUDENTS WORKING HARD TOGETHER.
DAB
DAB
THEN, TWO MONTHS AGO, THAT MURDERER APPEARED... AND NOW IT'S LIKE THIS.
ONE BY ONE, THE STUDENTS LEFT, FEARING THE NAME "BATTŌSAI."
THE TOWNSPEOPLE DON'T DARE COME NEAR.

EVEN NOW, IN THE MEIJI ERA, THE NAME "HITOKIRI BATTŌSAI" STRIKES FEAR.
WHY HE USES THE NAME KAMIYA KASSHIN-RYŪ...
AND IF HE REALLY IS BATTŌSAI...
...I HAVE NO IDEA. BUT WE HAVE TO STOP HIS KILLING SPREE AS SOON AS WE CAN.
TUP
MM. BUT YOU REALLY SHOULD STOP THIS PATROLLING AT NIGHT.
WHAT?
HE'S FAR STRONGER THAN YOU, KAORU-DONO.
RRR
HUH--?
A SWORDSMAN MUST BE HONEST ABOUT HIS FOE'S SKILL AND HIS OWN.
YOU SHOULD KNOW WHAT WILL HAPPEN NEXT TIME YOU FACE HIM.
IS THE PRESTIGE OF YOUR SCHOOL REALLY WORTH YOUR LIFE?

READ THIS WAY

KAMIYA KASSHIN-RYŪ--
--WAS DEVELOPED BY MY FATHER, WHO SURVIVED THE BAKUMATSU REVOLUTION.
HE REJECTED THE ETHICS OF *SATSUJIN-KEN*, "SWORDS THAT GIVE DEATH."
FOR TEN LONG YEARS, HE STRUGGLED TO CREATE A STYLE BASED ON *KATSUJIN-KEN*: "SWORDS THAT GIVE *LIFE*."
SIX MONTHS AGO, HE WAS DRAFTED FOR THE SEINAN WAR...AND LEFT THIS WORLD.
THIS HITOKIRI BATTŌSAI--
HAS MURDERED TEN PEOPLE IN OUR NAME.
KAMIYA KASSHIN-RYŪ--
MY FATHER'S IDEAL-- HIS LAST GIFT--HAS BEEN *DEFILED!*

BUT SUCH SHAME CANNOT BE UNDER-STOOD BY A MERE RUROUNI.
HEH.
BUT THAT ARM STILL SAYS NO NIGHT PATROL FOR A WHILE.
RK.
YOU SHOULD GET SOME REST NOW.
IF YOU REALLY BELIEVE IN KATSUJIN-KEN YOU HAVE A DUTY TO KEEP YOURSELF ALIVE.
KREE
AND ANY-WAY...

READ THIS WAY

READ THIS WAY

READ THIS WAY

OH, NOT ME!
NYAAA
......
WEAK IN BODY AND IN SPIRIT...
HUH?
OH, NOTHING.
SO YOU'RE STILL IN TOWN.
DO YOU HAVE SOME BUSINESS HERE?
UM... NOT EXACTLY ...
ANYWAY, HOW'S THE HUNT FOR THE MURDERER GOING?
OH... WELL...
I DO HAVE ONE LIKELY SUSPECT.
THERE'S A DOJO CALLED "KIHEIKAN" ON THE OUTSKIRTS OF THE NEXT TOWN OVER.
A DOJO ...?
NO.
MORE LIKE AN EX-DOJO. NOW IT'S A GATHERING PLACE FOR GAMBLERS AND ROGUES.

READ THIS WAY

A FORMER SAMURAI TOOK IT OVER ABOUT TWO MONTHS AGO.
A GIANT OF A MAN, THEY SAY-- 6 *SHAKU* 5 *SUN*.
1.95 meters-over 6 feet
HMM...
TWO MONTHS AGO. WHEN THE MURDERS STARTED.
THERE AREN'T MANY MEN THAT BIG. *AND* SKILLED WITH SWORDS.
I HAVE NO PROOF, SO I CAN'T DO ANYTHING...
BUT SOON...!
PAP
KAORU-SAN, I MUST LEAVE TO PREPARE DINNER.
OH. YES. THANK YOU.
YOU'LL EXCUSE ME--
THAT FELLOW WHO WAS WITH YOU BEFORE...
WHO, KIHEI?
HE'S A SORT OF LIVE-IN APPRENTICE.

READ THIS WAY
IT WAS RIGHT AFTER FATHER PASSED AWAY.
KIHEI COLLAPSED IN FRONT OF THE DOJO AND I HELPED HIM OUT.
HE DOESN'T REALLY BE-LIEVE IN GIRLS PRACTICING SWORDS-MANSHIP.
HE SAYS I SHOULD GIVE UP SWORDS, SELL THE DOJO, AND GO LIVE QUIETLY SOMEWHERE.
WHERE'S HE FROM?
I DON'T KNOW. I NEVER ASKED.
NEVER ASKED ?!
SHOULD I HAVE ?
WHY WOULD IT MAT-TER?
WE ALL HAVE THINGS IN OUR PASTS WE DON'T WANT TO TALK ABOUT.
YOU DO, DON'T YOU?
THAT'S WHY YOU'RE A RUROUNI.

READ THIS WAY

READ THIS WAY

READ THIS WAY

HELLO.
HELLO.
鬼兵館
KIHEIKAN
HELLO.
HELLO.
HELLO.
HELLO.
HELLO.
鬼兵館
HEL--
OH, SHUT UP! WHO ARE YOU?!
IS THE SENSEI ...?
MASTER HIRUMA IS OUT! COME BACK LATER!
AH, SO HIS NAME IS MASTER HIRUMA.
Y-YOU DIDN'T KNOW ...?
THIS ONE THOUGHT HIS NAME WAS...
"MURDERER BATTŌSAI."
RRG!

KAORU-DONO'S SUSPICIONS APPEAR CORRECT.
RATTLE
WHAT'S THE MATTER, NISHIWAKI?
TMP
WHO'S THE RUNT?
NOT EVEN A RUNT.
GET RID OF IT.

READ THIS WAY

......
RRG.
THE CUP CRACKED ...
KAORU-SAN.
EEK
KIHEI. YOU SCARED ME.
WHAT IS IT?
IT'S ABOUT SELLING THE PROPERTY, MISS.
?
KIHEI, I TOLD YOU I DON'T *WANT* TO SELL...
YES, MISS, BUT...
THE PAPERWORK IS ALREADY MADE UP.
DEED
KIHEI?
ALL I NEED NOW IS YOUR SEAL.

HEH
HELLO.
Y-YOU'RE --
TOOM
THEN THIS PROPERTY WILL BE OURS!
!
TOK
VSH
THIS IS MY BROTH-ER.
HIRUMA GOHEI, MASTER OF KIHEIKAN.

I DON'T LIKE TO DO IT THIS WAY.
I'D MUCH PREFER TO MAKE A *LEGAL* PURCHASE.
BUT SINCE YOU'VE CAUGHT ON TO MY BROTHER, I CAN'T TAKE CHANCES.
IT WAS ALL MOVING FORWARD QUITE NICELY, I THOUGHT. THE *KINDLY OLD MAN* TAKING CARE OF YOU AND GAINING YOUR *TRUST*...
UNFORTUNATELY FOR YOU, YOU ARE JUST SO *STUBBORN* ABOUT YOUR SWORD FIGHTING.
SO I USED MY BROTHER TO COOK UP THIS MURDER COMMOTION ...
AND DISCREDIT YOUR SCHOOL.
KIHEI ...
THE NAME "HITOKIRI BATTŌSAI" WORKED WONDERS.
THE LEGEND OF HIS TERRIBLE PROWESS IS SUCH THAT NO ONE DARED STAND AGAINST HIM.
師範
師範代
神谷薫
門下生
THANKS TO THAT, IT TOOK ONLY TWO MONTHS TO REDUCE YOU TO *THIS*.

READ THIS WAY

NKH!
VNNNNNN
!!
YOUR POWER IS ALL IN YOUR LITTLE-GIRL DREAMS.
HYO!
VOOO
KAH!

!!!
UHH ...
NN
TUG
MASTERY-- AND DEATH!
G ...
THAT IS WHAT A SWORD IS FOR!!
SSS

READ THIS WAY

NNN
DOMP
!?
RU...
RU-ROUNI...!
FORGIVE MY LATENESS.
HE TOLD ME EVERY-THING.
TUP

YOU AGAIN.
HSH
ARE YOU HERE TO TALK ABOUT "SWORDS THAT GIVE LIFE," TOO?!
.....
NO.
A SWORD IS A WEAPON.
SHE SPEAKS AS ONE WHO HAS NEVER BLOODIED HER HANDS.
KAORU-DONO MAINTAINS A SWEET, NAÏVE LIE.
WHATEVER PRETTY NAMES YOU GIVE IT, SWORDSMANSHIP IS A WAY TO KILL.
HENH
RU-ROUNI...

BUT IN THE FACE OF SUCH AWFUL TRUTH...
THE NAÏVE LIE SHE TELLS IS SO MUCH BETTER.
GLINT
IF THIS ONE HAD A WISH...
IT WOULD ONLY BE THAT HER LIE WOULD BECOME THE TRUTH OF THIS WORLD.
HEY, BRO. IT'S OKAY IF I KILL THIS GUY, RIGHT?
UH HUH.
HE'S BEEN A PAIN.
HAVE YOUR GOONS BEAT HIM TO DEATH.

READ THIS WAY
ALL RIGHT, BOYS?
YEAH!!
HSH
RUROUNI, PLEASE RUN!!
HURTING MORE PEOPLE SEEMS SO POINTLESS.
ANYONE WHO DISLIKES SEEING THE DOCTOR, LEAVE NOW.
THERE WILL BE NO WOUNDED...
...BUT RATHER, ONE DEAD BODY!!

ONE... SWING? IT CAN'T BE...
IS THIS SOME SORCERY ?!

NO...IT ISN'T SORCERY...
IT'S SPEED!
SPEED OF SWORD. SPEED OF BODY.
SPEED AT READING HIS OPPONENTS' MOVES. TAKING DOWN MAN AFTER MAN WITH THE LEAST POSSIBLE MOVEMENT!!
--OH.
ONE THING.

HITOKIRI BATTŌSAI DOESN'T USE KAMIYA KASSHIN-RYŪ...
...BUT AN ANCIENT STYLE OF THE SENGOKU ERA THAT PITS ONE AGAINST MANY..
...HITEN MITSURUGI-RYŪ.
IF NOT FOR SUCH A SWORD, THE BODY COUNT WOULD INCREASE TENFOLD.
!!! !!!
NO...
YOU... ARE THE HITOKIRI BATTŌSAI ...?
OH-HO!
!

READ THIS WAY
HSSSSS
SSSS
I THOUGHT YOU WERE NOBODY THE OTHER NIGHT. DIDN'T EVEN OCCUR TO ME TO FIGHT YOU.
NOW I REGRET IT!
UNLIKE YOU, THIS ONE DOESN'T CARE FOR VIOLENCE.
IF ONLY THIS HAD ENDED EARLIER.
QUITE REGRET-TABLE.
YOU'RE CONFIDENT ...
OR...
GLINT
...JUST VAIN.
THIS WORLD HAS NO ROOM--
FOR TWO BATTŌSAI! I AM THE ONE!!

!?
OVER HERE.

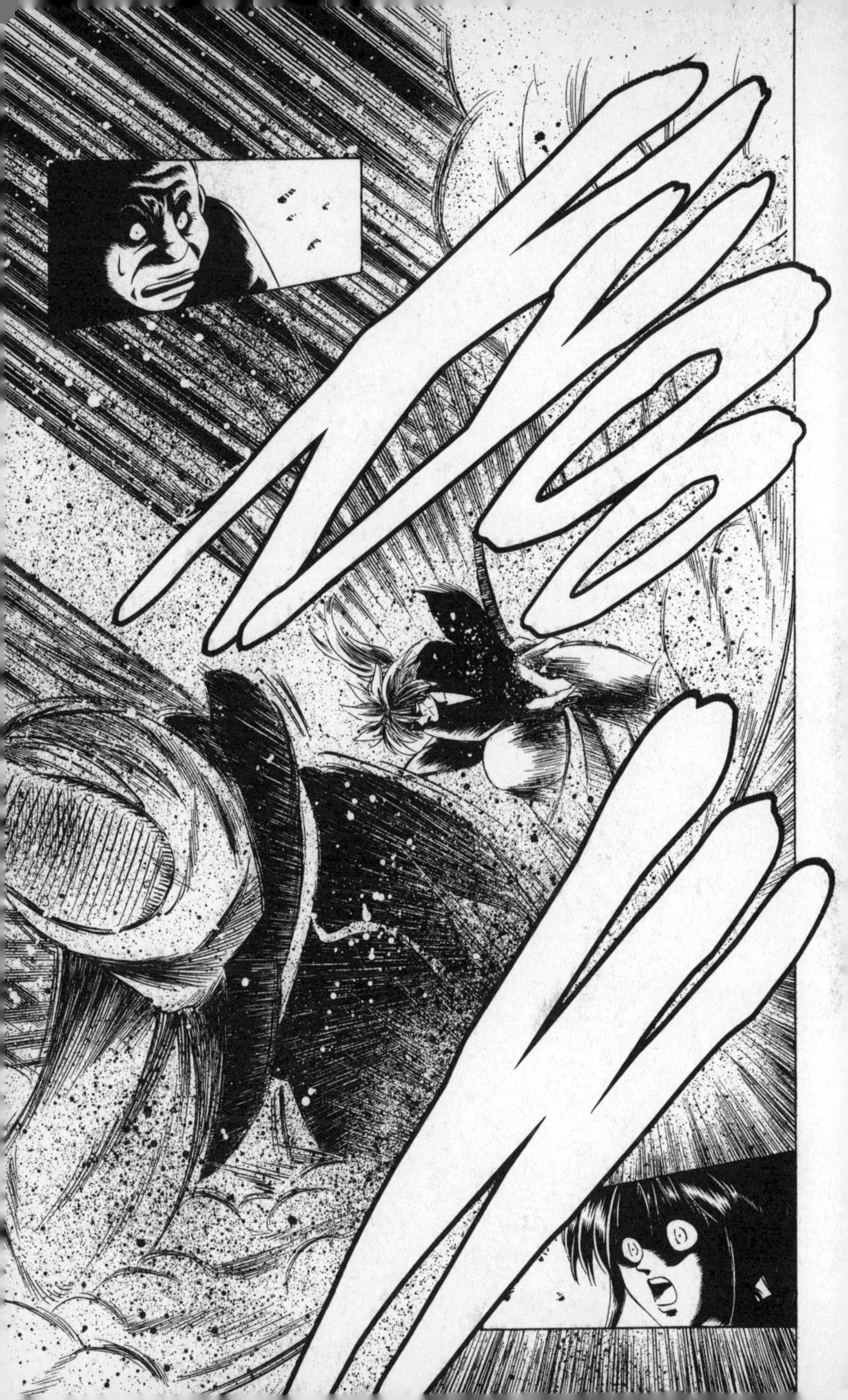

THIS ONE HAS NO ATTACHMENT TO THE NAME *BATTŌSAI.*
BUT STILL...THE LIKES OF YOU WON'T USE IT, EITHER.
TP TP
NOW. ONE LEFT.
THUD
!!
YOUR SOUL IS BLOODY EVEN IF YOUR HANDS ARE NOT.
CHK
SHALL WE TEST...
HIC
BRR BRR
HIC
...THE SHARPNESS OF THIS BLADE?
HHH
ZZZZ

READ THIS WAY

ZDDDD
PIDDLE PIDDLE
FEH.
THOSE WHO SEND OTHERS TO DEATH ARE USUALLY COWARDS.
RIP RIP
......
MY APOLOGIES, KAORU-DONO.
THIS ONE DID NOT WISH TO HIDE THE TRUTH.
BUT IT USUALLY IS BETTER...
...IF THIS ISN'T KNOWN.

B-BMP
EX-CUSE ME.
FARE-WELL ...
W...
W...
GRR
WAIT A SECOND!!
ORO ?
DO YOU THINK I'M GOING TO RUN THIS DOJO BY MYSELF ?!!
THE LEAST YOU COULD DO IS HELP ME OUT!!
I DON'T CARE WHO YOU USED TO BE!

READ THIS WAY

READ THIS WAY

FP
RATTLE
KENSHIN.
HIMURA KENSHIN.
THAT IS MY NAME... TODAY.
THIS ONE IS WEARY FROM TRAVELING.
THIS TALE BEGINS--
AS A RUROUNI, ONE NEVER KNOWS WHEN OR WHERE ONE WILL BE OFF TO NEXT...

--IN TOKYO IN THE 11TH YEAR OF MEIJI--
...BUT PLEASE EXCUSE THE INTRUSION FOR A LITTLE WHILE.
--WITH THE ARRIVAL OF THE RUROUNI, KENSHIN.
PING
HEY... WAIT A MINUTE...
IF YOU'RE A WARRIOR FROM THE BAKU-MATSU--
JUST HOW OLD ARE YOU?!
ORO?
AND WHAT'S "ORO" MEAN, ANYWAY?! YOU CAN'T BE OVER 30!! WITH A FACE LIKE THAT?!
EEEEEEEEEEEEEK
HOW OLD INDEED...
1
2
3--
YOU DON'T KNOW YOUR OWN AGE--?!!

READ THIS WAY

The Secret Life of Characters (1)

—Himura Kenshin—

Based somewhat on the actual *hitokiri, Kawakami Gensai.* Sort of. Except totally different.

Kawakami Gensai was one of the four great *hitokiri*, or assassins, of the revolutionary (Bakumatsu) period. He was short and skinny, and could be mistaken at first glance for a woman. Contrary to his appearance, though, he was clever and clear-headed despite also being most dreaded among all the *hitokiri.*

Master of an original sword-style called "Shiranui-ryū," Kawakami is famous for felling the great idealist Sakuma Shōzan in one swing, in mid-day. Kawakami is nevertheless a mysterious figure, however, as there are no certain records of his other assassinations.

After the revolution–and unable to let go of the idea that Japan should remain closed to the world–Kawakami found himself in frequent conflict with the revolutionary government. Ultimately, he was accused of a crime he did not commit and executed in the 4th year of Meiji.

As I researched further, it began to occur to me that the story wasn't so cut and dried. What this *hitokiri* could not let go of was his duty to his fallen comrades, and to the men that he had killed. It's this that gave me the initial idea for the "Kenshin" character. As for others, there is the selflessness of Okita Sōshi of the Shinsengumi and the mysterious quality of Saitō Hajime... but, then again, who knows.

In terms of graphic design, I had no real motif. The main character of my debut work was a tall, black-haired man in showy armor, so when I set out to design someone completely opposite to him, he ended up coming out like a girl (heh). Not knowing what else to do, I put a cross-shaped scar on the left cheek. Now that same cross marks the spot at which Battōsai became Kenshin...or so I've heard!

A WEEK HAS QUICKLY PASSED SINCE THE "BATTŌSAI" HOAX OF THE HIRUMA BROTHERS MET ITS END.
KAMIYA KAORU, MASTER OF THE KAMIYA KASSHIN-RYŪ DOJO, HAS BEEN RUNNING AROUND TRYING TO GET HER STUDENTS BACK.
神谷活心流
BUT...
NO ONE. NOT-- ONE.
RRR
RG
COWARDS!

Act 2 - Rurouni in the City

THESE ARE TIMES OF GREAT CHANGE.
ONCE THEY MOVE ON, IT'S NOT EASY TO COME BACK.
PAP
AND YOU! YOU SAY YOU'RE 28?!
IT'S A LIE AND YOU KNOW IT!
WOULD "30" MAKE YOU HAPPIER?
...NO, IT WOULDN'T ...
THIS ISN'T GOING TO BE EASY.

Act 2
Rurouni in the City

HIMURA KENSHIN IS A SWORDSMAN WITH NO DESTINATION, A "RUROUNI" WHO'S CURRENTLY STAYING AT MY DOJO.
BUT ONCE, HE WAS ONE OF THE REVOLUTIONARY WARRIORS WHO SLASHED OPEN THE NEW AGE...THE LEGENDARY, INCOMPARABLE HITOKIRI...
...HIMURA BATTOSAI HIMSELF.
OR SO HE SAYS...
THOB
ORO!
WHY IS HE A *RUROUNI*...
...WHILE ALL THE OTHER REVOLUTIONARIES THREW AWAY THEIR SWORDS...
...AND HAVE NOW TAKEN POSITIONS OF POWER AND GLORY IN THE MEIJI GOVERNMENT...?
HMM?

YOU HAVE A QUESTION IN YOUR EYES.
HEH
WE ALL HAVE THINGS IN OUR PASTS WE DON'T WANT TO TALK ABOUT.
......
RG
IT'S NOTHING!
PA
AND DIDN'T I TELL YOU NOT TO CARRY A SWORD?!
PA PA
PA
OWOH?
PA PA
CALM DOWN! JUST TWO YEARS AGO LOTS OF PEOPLE CARRIED SWORDS.
NO ONE'S REALLY BOTHERED BY IT, ARE THEY?
WHAT ARE YOU GONNA DO WHEN THE POLICE SPOT YOU LIKE LAST TIME?!
THEY'LL ARREST YOU EVEN IF IT IS A SAKABATŌ!
IT WORKED OUT LAST TIME, DIDN'T IT?
RRRRG.
LET'S JUST GET OUR SHOPPING DONE.
YOU GET THE MISO, SALT AND SOY SAUCE.
ALWAYS THE HEAVY THINGS.
NO COM-PLAIN-ING!
KLATTA KLATTA KLATTA KLATTA KLATTA KLATTA KLATTA
KIII

PLEASE PARDON OUR RUDENESS.
WE MUST ASK DIRECTIONS.
IS THIS THE CORRECT ROAD TO THE POLICE STATION?
!
UHHH...YES. TAKE A RIGHT ONTO THE MAIN STREET WHEN YOU HIT THE END.
THANK YOU.
LET US HURRY.
SCARED ME...
I WONDER WHO HE IS. I THINK I WOULD HAVE NOTICED...
KLATTA KLATTA
KLATTA KLATTA
KLATTA KLATTA
GAH. I HAVE TO FINISH SHOPPING!
TP TP TP
ARE YOU HERE?
ARE YOU TRULY IN THIS CITY...
...HIMURA BATTŌSAI?

READ THIS WAY
BLA BLA BLA
BLA BLA
WHAT'S THE COMMOTION?
WHAT HAP-PENED?
THE POLICE CAUGHT SOME GUY VIOLATING THE SWORD-BANNING ACT!
NK.
KRAK
YOU GAVE US A GOOD CHASE--
BUT NOW YOU'VE GOT NOWHERE TO RUN!!
VSSSSSSSH
HUF HUF HUF HUF HUF HUF HUF HUF HUF HUF
HMM... SO PERSISTENT.
WHAT CAN ONE DO BUT SURRENDER?
MOVE!!
LET THE SWORD CORPS THROUGH...
WOK
WAK
!!

TM
TM
THE POLICE SWORD CORPS. COMPOSED OF THOSE OFFICERS ADEPT WITH THE BLADE--AND TRUSTED BY THE GOVERNMENT TO CARRY ONE.
TMM
TMM
...OR OUR BLADES WILL MOVE YOU!
THERE'S REALLY NO NEED FOR THE SWORD CORPS TO...
BUT THE MAN HASN'T DRAWN HIS SWORD, AND WE HAVE HIM SURROUNDED.
GOOD JOB. WE WILL TAKE CARE OF IT. YOU ARE DISMISSED.
ZIP
LIEU-TENANT UJIKI...
A 3RD LIEU-TENANT WOULD TELL A VETERAN FROM SATSUMA WHAT TO DO?
WHEN I TELL YOU TO LEAVE, YOU LEAVE.
THOK!!!

WHAT IS THIS?
SUCH A GENTLE-LOOKING MAN.
FYOOOOOOOO
OH!
GASP
YOU MUST BE CONFIDENT TO BE CARRYING A SWORD HERE.
DRAW YOUR SWORD, GENTLE MAN.
THIS ONE DOES NOT CARRY A SWORD...
...MERELY TO FLAUNT IT AS A SYMBOL OF UNDESERVED POWER.

HMPH.
TOK
KENSHIN!
TM
TM
TM
TM
HUF
TM
TM
TM
SHE...
HM?
...IS WITH HIM?
KAORU-DONO, STAY AWAY!!
HUH?
ZASSSH

FFF
IT WILL BE MORE EMBARRASSING WHEN WE CUT HER KIMONO.
I'LL SAY IT AGAIN-- DRAW YOUR SWORD.
ARE YOU...
...REALLY A POLICEMAN?
AN OFFICER.
PERMITTED TO CARRY A SWORD.
A SWORDSMAN WHO CAN KILL PEOPLE LEGALLY.
WHAT'S THE MATTER? YOU AREN'T GOING TO DRAW?
.....
YOU TYRANT!
BOO
YOU AREN'T A GOD!
BOOO
GO BACK TO SATSUMA!

READ THIS WAY

DO NOT LAY A SINGLE BLADE...
ON ANY OF THESE CITIZENS.
THIS ONE IS YOUR OPPONENT.
IF YOU WANT DEATH, COME FORWARD.
AT LAST, HE TAKES THE BAIT.
WHATEVER I DO NOW IS CLEARLY SELF-DEFENSE.
CHK
HEH
TO STAY IN PRACTICE I NEED TO KILL SOMEONE EVERY ONCE IN A WHILE!!!

THEN IT WAS A HOAX...?
YES.
署長室
I WAS DELAYED BY THE MOPPING UP OF THE SEINAN WAR.
BUT HAD I THOUGHT IT OUT, I'D HAVE REALIZED THAT HIMURA WOULD NEVER USE HIS SWORD IN SUCH A MAD WAY.
IT IS TRUE THAT HE KILLED MANY IN EARNING THE NAME "HITOKIRI BATTŌSAI"...
BUT NEVER ONCE DID HE WIELD HIS SWORD IN SELF-INTEREST. ALL HE DID, HE DID FOR THE EMPEROR AND THE NEW ERA.
SSSS
SKRAK
HE SAVED THE LIVES OF MANY OF OUR WARRIORS.
WITHOUT HIM, THE REVOLUTION WOULD NOT HAVE SUCCEEDED.
WELL...WE FOUND THE CULPRITS OF THE HOAX TIED UP IN FRONT OF POLICE HEADQUARTERS EARLY ONE MORNING... WE DON'T KNOW WHO ARRESTED THEM. BUT...
WHEN WE INTERROGATED THE CULPRITS, THEY SAID, "THE *REAL* ONE GOT US."
WHAT...?!
OF COURSE, IT'S PROBABLY A LIE, BUT STILL...
PWIK

CHIEF!! THERE'S AN INCIDENT !!
BAMMM
I'M IN A MEETING, FOOL! AT LEAST KNOCK!!
MY APOLOGIES, SIR...
BUT THE SWORD CORPS IS...
UJIKI. IS HE CAUSING TROUBLE AGAIN?!
SWORD CORPS? I HAVEN'T HEARD OF THIS.
WE FORMED THEM TO HANDLE THIS "BATTŌSAI" INCIDENT...
BUT THEY ARE ALL BRUTAL MEN, AND THE CAPTAIN IS A REVOLUTIONARY WARRIOR FROM SATSUMA. IT'S TOO MUCH FOR ME TO HANDLE.
REVOLUTIONARIES WERE DIVIDED INTO FIVE CATEGORIES ACCORDING TO THEIR ORIGINS: SATSUMA (NOW KAGOSHIMA), CHŌSHŪ (YAMAGUCHI), TOSA (KŌCHI), HIZEN (SAGA), AND "OTHER" (MITO, FUKUOKA, ETC.).
SATSUMA AND CHŌSHŪ WERE THEN THE TWO GREATEST FORCES WITHIN THE MEIJI GOVERNMENT...
...SATSUMA IN THE POLICE FORCE AND CHŌSHŪ IN THE ARMY, DOMINATING THEM LIKE FEUDAL FIEFDOMS.
INDEED. A HERO FROM SATSUMA MUST SHOW OFF, MUSTN'T HE?
SO WHAT DID HE DO THIS TIME?
WELL... UMM...
THEY'RE GETTING BEATEN.
BY JUST ONE SWORDSMAN.

SHAK
WHAT? THAT'S IMPOSSIBLE!
THEY'RE THE FINEST SWORDSMEN IN OUR DEPARTMENT !!
BUT IT'S TRUE!
UNBELIEVABLE... WHO IS THIS MAN?
WE DON'T KNOW.
HE'S SHORT... SKINNY... YOUNG-LOOKING...
BUT HIS SWORD'S FASTER THAN THE EYE CAN SEE...
...AND HE HAS A SCAR LIKE A CROSS ON HIS CHEEK.
KLATTA KLATTA KLATTA KLATTA KLATTA KLATTA KLATTA KLATTA
HIMURA ...!
HSH

OH...!
TP
ONE LEFT.
RRR --

SWEAR THAT YOU WILL NOT TYRANNIZE YOUR PEOPLE ANY LONGER.
YAY
YAY
YAY
THEN WE CAN END THIS.
AND YOU MAY ARREST THIS ONE FOR VIOLATING THE SWORD-BANNING ACT.
SILENCE!
I CANNOT BOW TO YOU!!!
HIS STANCE...!
KYA
AAAA!
HE'S A MASTER OF JIGEN-RYŪ!
UJIKI, STOP! YOU'RE--
A DEAD FOOL.
JIGEN-RYŪ IS A STYLE OF UN-MATCHED POWER.
EXCEPT...

HYOHH!
DMM
...IN THE FACE OF HITEN MITSURUGI-RYU.

GOOD JOB, MAN!
WHERE ARE YOU FROM?!
!
ORO!
LET'S GO GRAB A DRINK!
SWOOSH
KENSHIN!
TM TM TM
ARE YOU ALL RIGHT?
HIMURA.
I'VE FINALLY FOUND YOU.
TUP
FOR TEN YEARS I'VE SOUGHT YOU...
CHIEF, PLEASE HAVE THE PEOPLE MOVE ALONG.
RIGHT!
THE YAMAGATA...? REALLY...?
YOU'VE GROWN A MUSTACHE, YAMAGATA-SAN.

MOVE ALONG, MOVE ALONG.
TYRANTS!
HEY, MAN, BEAT THESE GUYS, TOO!
GENERAL OF THE REVOLUTIONARY ARMY'S "KIHEITAI"...NOW GENERAL OF THE ARMY'S GROUND TROOPS...
THE REVOLUTIONARY WARRIOR, YAMAGATA ARITOMO!
I HAVE A CARRIAGE WAITING.
SSSS
MANY OF YOUR COMRADES AWAIT YOUR RETURN.
COME!
MY APOLOGIES, BUT...
!!
WHAT ARE YOU SAYING?! YES, YOU KILLED --BUT IT WAS ALL FOR THE REVOLUTION!
YOUR SOUL BEARS NO BURDEN!!
...NOT ONE STRAND OF HAIR ON MY BODY WISHES TO SPEND THE REST OF MY LIFE AS A HITOKIRI.
ONLY COWARDS AND FOOLS WOULD DENOUNCE YOU AS A "HITOKIRI"!
BUT I WILL--

READ THIS WAY

WITH A SWORD, THE PEOPLE WITHIN MY SIGHT...
...CAN AT LEAST BE PROTECTED.
PM
THIS ONE IS NO DIFFERENT NOW FROM BEFORE.
EXCEPT THAT HE IS NOW A "RUROUNI" AND NOT A "HITOKIRI."
......
CHIEF ...
I KNOW. IT'S CLEAR WHO WAS AT FAULT HERE.
AND A SWORD WORN OPENLY IS SAFER THAN CONCEALED.
SIGH
I WON'T PURSUE THIS.
AFTER THAT HOAX I THOUGHT THAT HITOKIRI BATTŌSAI...
...WAS A DANGEROUS FIGURE. BUT NOW...

...NOW I KNOW THE TRUTH IS DIFFERENT.
MY APOLOGIES, KAORU-DONO.
I THINK I UNDERSTAND...
YOU DO?
YOUR HAIR RIBBON. IT WAS RUINED BECAUSE OF ME.
..AT LEAST A LITTLE MORE.
HE WANTS TO PROTECT PEOPLE, WITHOUT BEING TIED TO ANYONE.
DON'T WORRY ABOUT IT. YOU CAN JUST DO SOME EXTRA HOUSEWORK!
......
A RUROUNI. A HERO. BUT FREE IN SPIRIT.
白みそ
CARRYING ALL THIS ISN'T ENOUGH?
DID YOU REALLY HAVE TO BUY IT ALL AT ONCE?
MAYBE NOT.

READ THIS WAY

The Secret Life of Characters (2)

—Kamiya Kaoru—

No specific model here. If pressed, I'd probably have to say the character Chiba Sanako from the novel *"Ryōma no Koibito"*—the self-proclaimed "Ryōma's Girl." There's also that "commanding" quality which I tried to incorporate of Sasaki Mifuyu in *"Kenkyaku Shōbai"* by novelist Ikenami Shōtarō...but Kaoru wound up a plain, regular girl regardless. (Ah, well.)

As it turns out, though, "just plain Kaoru" seems to be working out for now, so I can't complain. Certainly many of my female readers seem to be relating to her. Some of them write that they can't tell if she's "strong" or "weak" as a fighter, but the truth is that she *is* strong.

Kaoru is quite independent for her age, and can hold her own against the kendō masters of the many dojos in town. That makes her at very least a national-level champion. If Kaoru does appear weak, it's only because Kenshin and Sanosuke are so powerful. Whether or not she'll become Kenshin's love interest in the future, even I haven't quite yet decided.

Design-wise, there's no real motif here, either. You could say her look was inevitable. For a girl involved in kendō, after all, a ponytail is *de rigeur.* (Heh.) A blade, a kimono, a ponytail...what's not to like, right? Drawing her is enjoyable enough, although filling in her hair is sometimes a pain.

In that I am a "men, glorious and women, cute" kind of guy, it's true that ideally I'd like Kaoru to be drawn a bit more cutely. "Down-to-Earth" and "poor" are also parts of her character, though, and I can't overlook that. I do wish I could improve the pattern of her kimono, and let her be at least a little more fashionable.

Act 3
Tokyo Samurai

THE DAY AFTER KENSHIN CRUSHED THE SWORD CORPS ...
THE WORD WAS OUT AND THE DOJO WAS PACKED.
YADA
YADA
YADA
WOW! 15 PEOPLE!!
1
2
3...
WE'LL HAVE KAMIYA KASSHIN-RYŪ BACK IN NO TIME!
THIS ISN'T GOOD...
HUH?
HEY EVERYONE.
THIS ONE IS NOT FROM THIS DOJO, AND IS TAKING NO STUDENTS.
YADA
YADA
SO IF YOU ARE HERE BECAUSE OF YESTERDAY'S INCIDENT...
...PLEASE GO HOME.
GOOD, GOOD.
...
TP TP
NOW, TIME TO HEAT UP THE BATH.
HWOOOOO

IDIOT!
WHY DID YOU SEND THEM HOME?!!
TAKING ON STUDENTS IS NOT...
WHY DO THEY HAVE TO KNOW THAT?!
GGGGGG
ONCE I'VE GOT 'EM IN, I'LL MAKE SURE THEY STAY!!
THAT WOULD BE DIS-HONEST.
AARGH!
ARE YOU STILL MAD?
15 STUDENTS! 15 STUDENTS!
BUT THRILL-SEEKERS LIKE THAT NEVER LAST EVEN SIX MONTHS.
THAT'S NOT WHAT YOU WANT.
...
RRR
THERE'S NO NEED TO RUSH.
JUST HAVE PATIENCE, AND OPTI-MISM!

BUT I CAN'T DO ANY TRAINING WITHOUT VISITING SOMEBODY ELSE'S DOJO, BECAUSE I DON'T HAVE ANY STUDENTS TO TRAIN WITH!
AND YOU WON'T SPAR WITH ME!
MY SKILL WITH A PRACTICE SWORD IS LACKING.
TM TM TM TM TM TM TM TM TM TM TM
ORO!
B
MP
STOP!
HO!
KENSHIN-- THIS KID'S A PICK-POCKET!!
THIS IS YOUR WALLET, YEAH?!!
TINKLE

LEGGO!
LET ME GO, UGLY!!
ARRH
YOU, UGLY!
YOWL
YOWL
YOWL
WH...
WHO'RE YOU CALLING UGLY, STUPID?!
IF HE NEEDS THIS SO BADLY...
WAIT. WAIT.
YOUNG ONE.
DON'T GET CAUGHT NEXT TIME.
GGG
LET'S GO.
W-WAIT A MINUTE!
TP

KLONNG
!
ORO!
I'M NOT A "YOUNG ONE"!!
I'M MYŌJIN YAHIKO-- TOKYO SAMURAI!
I HAVEN'T FALLEN FAR ENOUGH TO BE PITIED BY STRANGERS!!
YOUNG ONE...
I'M NOT A YOUNG ONE!!
I WAS JUST TESTING YOU BECAUSE YOU HAD A SWORD!
DON'T GET THE WRONG IDEA!
MRR...
YOU LOOK LIKE A CHILD BUT IT'S OBVIOUS THAT YOUR SOUL IS MATURE.
SORRY. DIDN'T MEAN TO UNDER-ESTIMATE YOU.

READ THIS WAY

......
HMPH.
TM TM TM
WOULD YOU SAY HE'S PROUD OR ASHAMED?
I'D SAY HE'S A BRAT.
POOR BOY...
IF THE WORLD WERE LIKE IT WAS, HE'D HAVE JOINED THE TRULY GREAT SAMURAI...
SHFF
HEY. THERE HE IS.
HEH
WE HAD TO GO LOOKING FOR YOU, YAHIKO.

READ THIS WAY

READ THIS WAY

MMM... THAT WAS A GOOD SWEAT.
NOW I'LL JUST GET HOME, HAVE SOME TEA, AND...
HEY, I WONDER IF KENSHIN FIRED UP THE BATH?
K-KLO
K-KLA
HE WENT HOME EARLY, SO HE SHOULD ...
HUH.
THAT'S ...!
関東集英組
HNH.
STUBBORN PUNK.
PLUP
PLUP

READ THIS WAY
ALL YOU GOT TO SAY IS *YOU'RE SORRY.*
EASE UP FOR A MINUTE, GASUKE.
OR THERE WON'T BE ANYTHING LEFT TO *APOLOGIZE.*
YEAH RIGHT
BOSS...
YAHIKO, HOW DO YOU THINK YOU'RE GOING TO *LIVE* IF YOU QUIT THIEVING?
IF YOU THINK YOU'LL BE FINE SOMEHOW BE-CAUSE YOU'RE OF SAMURAI DESCENT, THEN YOU'RE WRONG.
THIS NEW WORLD OF OURS IS ALL ABOUT *MONEY.*
PRIDE ISN'T WORTH A THING.
WHEN SAMURAI HANG ON TO THEIR PRIDE, IT ONLY PULLS THEM DOWN DEEPER.
THE BROTHELS ARE OVER-FLOWING WITH THE WIVES AND DAUGHTERS OF "PROUD" SAMURAI.
AND WHENEVER A GANG OF BAN-DITS IS CAUGHT, YOU KNOW WHO *THEY* WERE IN FORMER LIFE.
AAAAA
IT'S PITIFUL.

FORGET THIS "NOBLE LINEAGE," YAHIKO. LEARN TO LIVE A HUMBLE LIFE.
THEN I'LL TAKE YOU IN. TANISHI'S MAN...THAT'S SOMETHING TO BE *PROUD* OF.
DON'T MAKE ME REPEAT IT:
I DECLINE.
PEH
WHO ARE *YOU* SPITTIN' AT?! THE BOSS WHO *TOOK CARE* O'YOU SINCE YOUR PARENTS DIED?!
MNCH
MNCH
YOU DOG!
DON'T LIE TO YOURSELF.
YOU CALL YOURSELF A SAMURAI, BUT WHAT DID YOUR DAD EVER HAVE? THREE ACRES AND TWO SERVANTS!
AND THEN THE MORON TRIED TO FIGHT THE REVOLUTION AND GOT HIMSELF *KILLED!*
YOUR MOTHER HAD TO SELL HER *BODY* IN A *BROTHEL* AND DIED OF SYPHILIS!
WHICH DO *YOU* TAKE AFTER? THE *FOOL* OR THE *WHORE?*

SHUT UP!!
GOMP!!
!
....
....
YEEAAA!
GA-SUKE-SAN!
DOOF
MY FATHER DIED FAITHFUL TO HIS LORD, OPPOSING A REVOLUTION THAT HE KNEW WAS IMMORAL.
GRN
GRN
MY MOTHER WORKED TO PUT FOOD ON MY TABLE, TO RAISE ME WELL, UNTIL IT KILLED HER.

THEY LIVED AND DIED AS SAMURAI!
I WON'T FORGIVE ANYONE WHO INSULTS THEM!!
I'M THE ONE THAT WON'T FORGIVE, PUNK!
SHING
I'M GONNA KILL Y--
DMM

ZUDD
!?
TROOM
WH...
WHO THE HELL ARE YOU?!!
!
IT'S A RAID!! GET THE GUYS!!
THEY WON'T COME.
THEY WEREN'T GOING TO LET ME IN, SO I HAD THEM GO TO SLEEP FOR A LITTLE WHILE.

READ THIS WAY
WH...
I AM HIMURA KENSHIN, A RUROUNI.
I'VE COME FOR THE YOUNG ONE.
HSH
WHAT ARE YOU--
ANOTHER SAMURAI FOOL?!
I'LL KILL YOU BOTH AT--
ONCE?!

WE'RE TALKING.
JUST STAY THERE AND BE QUIET FOR A WHILE.
PLUK
PLUK
PLUK
PLUK
......
SHIK
WHAT DO YOU SAY?
SHOW YOUR GENEROSITY AND RELEASE THE YOUNG ONE.
BRRR
IT MAY EMBARRASS YOU LESS THAN THE TOTAL ANNIHILATION OF YOUR GANG...
FINE. GO AHEAD AND TAKE HIM.
THANK YOU.
PLEASE FORGIVE THE INTRUSION.
KING
ARE YOU ALL RIGHT, YOUNG ONE?
YOU WERE HARD TO PINPOINT, BUT AFTER VISITING ONE YAKUZA GROUP AFTER ANOTHER...
TP

SLAP
I COULD HAVE FOUGHT !!
I COULD HAVE FOUGHT THEM ALONE!
WHO TOLD YOU TO HELP ME?
THIS ONE HAS UNDER-ESTIMATED YOU ONCE AGAIN.
...OF COURSE.
SWOOP
THEN, AS AN APOLOGY, AT LEAST ALLOW YOUR WOUNDS TO BE TREATED.

YOU WON'T GET AWAY!
NO! DON'T MIND THEM!
THOSE WERE THE EYES OF A "HITOKIRI."
AND NOT A *HITOKIRI* FROM THE YAKUZA. THAT'S A REAL ONE.
I DIDN'T KNOW THERE WERE STILL MEN *LIKE* THAT.
NO NUMBER OF MEN WOULD BE ENOUGH AGAINST HIM.
IF ONE KID IS ALL IT TAKES, IT'S A CHEAP PRICE.
...DAMN.
DAMN.
DAMN.
DAMN.
DAMN.

ARE YOU THAT BOTHERED BY YOUR LACK OF POWER...
...YOUNG ONE?
DAMN.
I WANT TO BE STRONG.
SO STRONG I WON'T NEED YOUR HELP...
STRONG ENOUGH TO DEFEND MY FATHER AND MOTHER'S PRIDE ON MY OWN...
.....
OF COURSE ...
HE'S TAKING A LONG TIME ...
I'M SURE KENSHIN'S OKAY, BUT...
...WHAT ABOUT THE BOY...?

READ THIS WAY

READ THIS WAY

YEP. ♡
.....
THE STAGE HAS BEEN SET...
PAT
...THE REST IS UP TO YOU.
YOU CAN BE AS STRONG AS YOU WANT, YAHIKO.
AND SO...
...THE 2ND RESIDENT OF KAMIYA DOJO...
HEH!
YOU DON'T NEED TO TELL ME!
...TOKYO SAMURAI MYŌJIN YAHIKO... CAME TO JOIN US.
YOU'RE GONNA STOP CALLING ME UGLY!
SPEW
WHY SHOULD I, UGLY?!
SPEW
SHOULDN'T WE BE GOING TO THE DOCTOR ...?

READ THIS WAY

The Secret Life of Characters (3)

—Myōjin Yahiko—

More than any historical reality, the character of Yahiko grew out of feelings I had in middle school. I was in the kendō club—at first just because it was something to do—but then I got hooked on it as much as drawing manga, and soon I was swinging the *shinai* every day to the point of exhaustion.

The problem, though, was that I was weak. So weak, in fact, that I was an embarrassment to my 183 centimeters of height! In three years of middle school, I was a member of a starting squad only once, and then only because the kid who was *supposed* to be a starter got suspended for causing trouble, and I got bumped up by luck of the draw. Even then, still I was unable to score a win in a league tournament.

The disgrace I felt at kendō, the wanting to be stronger, the still being awful no matter how much I longed to be great, all of that has found an outlet in little Yahiko. Yahiko knows a pain that hero-types like Kenshin and Sanosuke can never know. Of late, he's turned more into a comedic character, but still my wish is to draw him in such a way that, five or ten years down the road, readers can envision him as a great swordsman.

As with Kaoru, there's no particular logic in Yahiko's design...that is, of course, unless you consider that having a defiant-eyed young man with mussed hair is itself a must in a comic for young men.

Act 4 - Kasshin-Ryū Reborn

KENSHIN, YOU TELL HIM!
THEN WASH OUT HIS MOUTH!
FOO!!
PING!
I'M HERE TO BECOME STRONG!
NOT TO TRAIN AGAINST SOME LITTLE GIRL!
"LITTLE" ...!!
KENSHIN, YOU TOLD ME TO GET STRONGER.
YOU TEACH ME!
THE HITEN MITSURUGI-RYŪ WILL NOT BE PASSED ON TO THE NEXT GENERATION ...
THIS ONE IS JUST AN OBSERVER.
YOU SHOULD BECOME STRONG WITH KAMIYA KASSHIN-RYŪ... AND KATSUJIN-KEN.
THEY'RE NOT EVEN LISTENING.
I'LL STRAN-GLE YOU!!
I DARE YOU!!

Act 4
Kasshin-Ryū Reborn

HYOH!
HUF
HUF
HUF
STOP!!
DMDMDMDMDMDMDMDM
...
...
YAHIKO...
YAHIKO...
YAHIKO!!
HE'S BEEN SKIPPING OUT SINCE THE 2ND DAY...
......
KCHING
FILTHY MOUTH, STUBBORN PERSON-ALITY, AND NO GUTS.
WHAT DID KENSHIN SEE IN HIM?
GOOSH

READ THIS WAY

SATŌ-KUN TOO! HOW DID YOU GET THAT WOUND?!
WHAT HAPPENED ?!
GNK
YOU CAN'T GET AWAY NOW--
I'LL KILL YOU!
!
WHO ARE YOU?!
AND WHAT ARE YOU DOING TO MY FORMER STUDENTS?!
SHUT UP AND GET OUTTA THE WAY.
VSH
AUGH!
FYEW

...
WHAT'S THE MEANING OF THIS?
HUF
HUF
EXPLAIN THIS TO ME!
WELL, UMM...WE RAN INTO A GANG OF DRUNKS IN THE CITY...
YEAH, AND THEY WERE BOTHERING PEOPLE, SO WE TOOK THEM DOWN, BUT...
...THEN THEIR FRIENDS SHOWED UP...
...AND SAID SOMETHING ABOUT REVENGE...
WHERE'D THEY GO?!
THERE!

THERE THEY ARE!
!
BOOOOOOOOM
S...SO MANY...
OHHH
THERE ARE TOO MANY OF THEM!
EVERYONE INTO THE DOJO!!
TM TM TM TM TM TM
HUF HUF
WHAT THE ...?
BTAM
CRAP.
MASTER HACHI-SUKA!
HEH. HOW NICE.
SHOW THEM WHAT HAPPENS TO THOSE WHO OPPOSE THE HISHI-MANJI GUREN GANG!
KKK

WHO ARE THEY?
THE HISHIMANJI GUREN GANG-- NOW I GET IT.
A BAND OF DELINQUENTS-- LIKE AN ARMY RESERVE FOR CRIMINALS.
THEY CAN BE MORE DANGEROUS THAN THE YAKUZA BECAUSE THEY'VE GOT LESS TO LOSE.
WELL, WE ARE IN TROUBLE. WHY DOES THIS HAVE TO HAPPEN WHEN KENSHIN IS GONE?
AUGH!
THAT'S WHY I HAVEN'T SEEN HIM! WHERE'D HE GO?
I ASKED HIM TO GO SHOPPING FOR RICE, SALT, MISO, SOY SAUCE...
IDIOT...
DO YOU HAVE TO BUY THEM ALL AT ONCE?
WHAT SHOULD WE DO, KAORU-SAN?
WHAT DO YOU MEAN, "WE"? YOU FOOLS STARTED IT!
THEY'RE NOT AT FAULT HERE.
I'LL SAY IT AGAIN: "IDIOT."
YOU DON'T REALLY BELIEVE THEIR STORY, DO YOU?
!?

OR MAYBE YOU DIDN'T NOTICE THE STENCH OF ALCOHOL ON THEIR BREATH.
......!
YOU WERE THE ONES WHO GOT DRUNK AND STARTED ROUGHING PEOPLE UP.
WEREN'T YOU? AND THEN YOU PICKED A *FIGHT* WITH SOME HISHIMANJI THUGS!
IS THAT TRUE?
......
WELL? IS IT?
I'M SORRY ...
KABOOOM
!?

HYAA HAHA HA! WALLS ARE NOTHING TO HISHI-MANJI!
COME ON OUT!
OR I'LL DEMOLISH THIS CRAPPY DOJO!
PUFF
PUFF
WOODEN CANNON: A SIMPLE CANNON MADE OF OAK, LAUNCHING BALLS OF CLAY. ITS POWER WAS COMPARABLE TO NORMAL CANNONS.
FUFF
A WOODEN CANNON ...!
HOW CAN THEY HAVE A THING LIKE THAT?!
FUFF
FUFF
NEVER BE SURPRISED BY HISHI-MANJI.
WE DON'T DEPEND ON MEASLY SWORDS.
NOW TO SETTLE THE SCORE FOR MY GUY WHO GOT HIS ARM BROKEN...

READ THIS WAY
YOU GUYS USED YOUR SWORDS FOR A DRUNKEN FIGHT...
...AND HURT PEOPLE?
......
BRR
BRR
BRR
BRR
THEY MAY BE CRUDE AND STUPID...
...BUT YOU GUYS ARE EVEN WORSE!
BESIDES, "FORMER STUDENTS" MEANS YOU GUYS RAN AWAY WITH YOUR TAILS BETWEEN YOUR LEGS WHEN THINGS GOT TOUGH--
AND NOW YOU RUN BACK TO THE DOJO FOR HELP?!
DOOM
YOU CAN'T GET AWAY NOW.
COME OUT!
HEEE!

READ THIS WAY

READ THIS WAY

DO NOT TAKE ME, MYŌJIN YAHIKO, FOR SCUM LIKE THIS!
DO YOU THINK I COULD LET YOU DIE ALONE?
YOU BRAT!
NOW I WON'T LET YOU GO! I'LL KILL YOU!
RRR
THAT DOESN'T SOUND VERY FRIENDLY...
!?
KENSHIN!
PERHAPS THE TWO IN THE BACK HAVE BEEN UP TO NO GOOD, BUT STILL. DID YOU HAVE TO RESORT TO A CANNON?
CLOK
NOW LET'S CALM DOWN AND WORK THIS OUT.

READ THIS WAY
AND WHO THE HELL ARE YOU?!!
MASTER HACHISUKA, THIS IS BAD. THIS GUY IS...IS...
REMEMBER THE RUROUNI WHO BEAT UP THE POLICE SWORD CORPS BY HIMSELF?
I THINK IT'S HIM.
COWARD! YOU GONNA LET YOURSELF BE SCARED BY ONE RUROUNI?!
GNNNNNNN
WE HAVE THIS ON OUR SIDE. PREPARE THE CANNON!
NNHH!!
FIRE!
!
YEAH !!

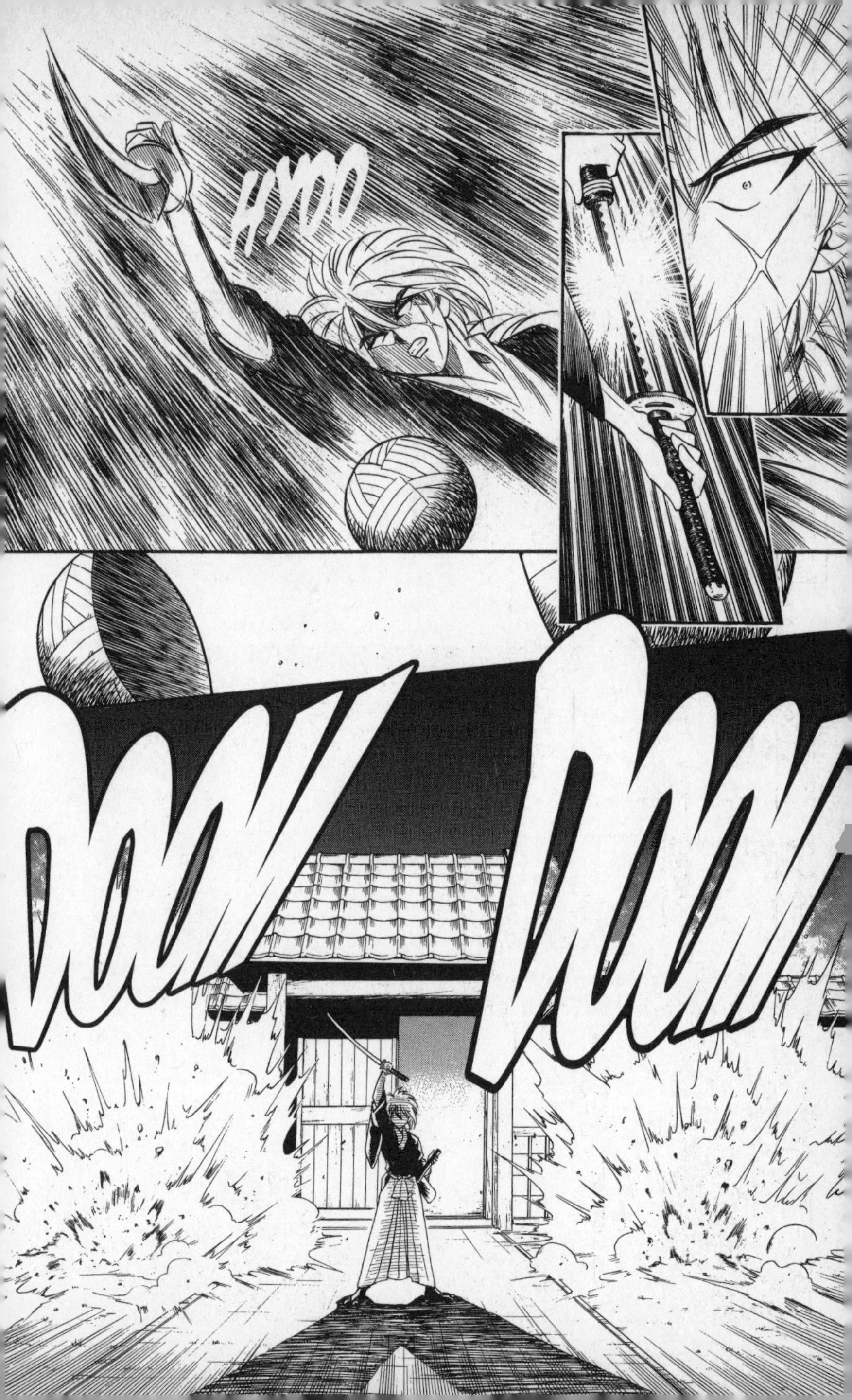
HYOO

READ THIS WAY
IT'S POINTLESS TO HESITATE...
.....
...WHEN USING THIS SAKABATŌ AGAINST NON-HUMAN OBJECTS.
ONCE AGAIN. STOP THIS FOOLISHNESS.
MY, MY.
SO MUCH HAPPENS WHEN THIS ONE IS AWAY.
UMM ...
IT DOESN'T MATTER. GO HOME NOW.
AND FORGET FROM THIS MOMENT ON THAT YOU WERE STUDENTS OF THIS PLACE.
NEVER HOLD A SWORD IN YOUR HANDS AGAIN.
.....
HIRA-CHAN...
PWIK

THE WOUND ON YOUR SHOULDER... MAKE SURE YOU GO SEE A DOCTOR...
......
BOW BOW
CHEER UP, KAORU-DONO.
PAT
NO MATTER HOW SINCERELY YOU TRY...
...THERE ARE TIMES WHEN YOUR THOUGHTS JUST DON'T REACH THE STUDENT.
QUIT CRYING. IT DOESN'T SUIT YOU.
TP TP TP TP TP TP TP
I WON'T TURN OUT LIKE THEM.
!

I KNOW IT'S IMPOSSIBLE TO BE LIKE KENSHIN RIGHT AWAY.
SO I'LL SETTLE FOR YOUR LEVEL FOR NOW.
I'LL ENTER YOUR DOJO.
THERE ARE THOSE YOU REALLY DO REACH.
HEH
BUT THEN...
ZIP
THIS EARLY SPRING DAY IN THE 11TH YEAR OF MEIJI, THE FIRST SMALL STEP WAS TAKEN.
KAMIYA KASSHIN-RYŪ. NO MASTER. ONE INSTRUCTOR, KAMIYA KAORU. ONE STUDENT, MYŌJIN YAHIKO. AND A RUROUNI, HIMURA KENSHIN.
I'VE GOT NO TIME TO FOOL AROUND! KAORU! HURRY UP AND ATTACK ME!
I WANT TO GET GOOD AS FAST AS I CAN!!
I LIKED IT BETTER WHEN YOU CALLED ME UGLY.

Rurouni Kenshin
Meiji Swordsman
Romantic Story
Nobuhiro Watsuki
るろうに剣心
—明治剣客浪漫譚—
和月伸宏

OHHH...
W-WE... WE GIVE UP. YOU'RE TOO GOOD. FORGIVE US.
YOU DON'T HAVE TO TELL ME TO STOP.
!?
YOU'RE TOO WEAK FOR ME!
TSK
IF I KEEP GOING, I'LL LOOK LIKE A BULLY.
WHAT A BORING FIGHT I BOUGHT...

Act 5
The Fight Merchant

Act 5
The Fight Merchant

SO I SAID, WE DON'T HAVE TO WORRY ABOUT EX-PENSES FOR A WHILE.
I FOUND IT WHILE I WAS ORGANIZING THE CLOSET!
MY GRAMPA DREW...
TA-DAA
AHH... DOODLING.
INK PAINTING !!!
MY GRAMPA WASN'T JUST A SWORDSMAN, HE WAS A MASTER OF PAINTING IN INK.
I CAN SELL THIS FOR A LOT OF MONEY.
OH, THANK YOU, GRAMPA!
WOMEN AND CASH.
AND NOW WE'RE GONNA SPLURGE AT THE BEEF-POT HOUSE FOR LUNCH!
HEY! I SAID YOU COULD TEACH ME SWORDS! NOTHING ELSE!

THE CULTURAL RENAISSANCE OF MEIJI ALSO HAD A GREAT INFLUENCE ON JAPANESE CUISINE, CREATING A VARIETY OF NEW DISHES.
AMONG THEM, BEEF-POT OR GYŪNABE (SUKIYAKI) WAS SEEN AS REPRESENTATIVE OF EUROPEAN FOODS, AND WAS AFFORDABLE TO THE GENERAL PUBLIC.
RATTLE
BLAH BLAH BLAH BLAH
BLAH BLAH BLAH BLAH
BLAH BLAH BLAH BLAH
BLAH BLAH BLAH
HELLO, AND COME ON--
KAORU-CHAN! COME IN!!
LONG TIME NO SEE, TAE-SAN.
YOU LOOK GOOD.
AND YOU'VE SOME UN-FAMILIAR FACES WITH YOU TODAY.
THAT GUY OVER THERE YOUR LOVER?
NO, JUST A GUEST OF THE DOJO.
I DON'T BELIEVE IT!!

!?
WE WILL NEVER GAIN OUR RIGHTS THROUGH SUCH METHODS! ONLY A FAR MORE RADICAL...
BLAH BLAH
BUT THAT WILL BE JUST LIKE SENDING MASTER ITAGAKI TO HIS DEATH.
THEIR HOME SECRETARY, ŌKUBO IS A MAN WHO DIDN'T HOLD BACK ON THE GREAT SAIGŌ!
BLAH BLAH
ŌKUBO IS FINE. WHO WOULDN'T WANT TO BE PLEASED TO DIE AND BECOME A LEGEND LIKE SAIGŌ?
YADA
YADA
FOOL. THERE'S NOTHING TO GAIN FROM THE ROMANCE OF "BECOMING A LEGEND."
IF MASTER ITAGAKI DIES, FREEDOM WILL ALSO DIE!!
THOSE GUYS. THEY ALWAYS GET LIKE THAT WHEN THEY'RE DRUNK.
ACTIVISTS OF THE DEMOCRATIC RIGHTS MOVEMENT, IT SOUNDS LIKE.
SOUNDS LIKE GIBBERISH TO ME.
JUST A BUNCH OF DRUNKS.
WELL, DON'T MIND THEM. FOR THREE, THEN, IS IT?
OH, AND THREE "COFFEE" PLEASE.
BLAH
BLAH
BLAH
BLAH
.....!
....
......!!
.....
!

READ THIS WAY

READ THIS WAY

OH!
!
WELL, NOW.
AREN'T THE DEFENDERS OF HUMAN RIGHTS SUPPOSED TO PROTECT THE WEAK?
OR ARE THE RIGHTS YOU SPEAK OF...
HEH
...THE RIGHTS TO GET DRUNK AND VIOLENT?

READ THIS WAY
WHAT DID YOU SAY?!
OHH!
ARE YOU CHALLENGING US ?!
ARE YOU ALL RIGHT?
UM... YES.
WELL, I SUPPOSE I WILL "SELL" FOR A CHANGE.
I'M USUALLY THE ONE WHO "BUYS," BUT...
I DON'T LIKE THOSE WHO PICK ON THE WEAK.
ESPECIALLY THOSE WHO BARK OUT PRETTY WORDS LIKE FREEDOM, JUSTICE, AND EQUALITY.
NOTHING SICKENS ME LIKE A HYPOCRITE!
ARRRH!
POP POP POP POP POP POP POP POP POP
STEP OUTSIDE !!

赤べこ
WHAT A WEIRD SITUATION...
WOULD IT BE BEST TO STOP THEM?
HE WANTED TO DO IT, SO MAYBE NOT.
I'LL SHOW NO MERCY, EVEN IF YOU CRY.
KRAK KRAK
LET'S SEE WHAT YOU'VE GOT.
COME AT ME.
PING PING
FOOL!
OHOOOO

SHP
HEH
TAKE THIS!!
COWARD! HIDING A SUN-TETSU!
A BAD THING, INDEED...
AW, SHUT IT!!
A SUNTETSU IS *MEANT* TO BE A CONCEALED WEAPON!!
HOW-EVER...
...IT MAKES NO DIFFER-ENCE.
FEH...

THAT'S IT? EVEN WITH THE SUN-TETSU?
YOU DISAPPOINT ME.
KIIIN
AA AA-AAAAA!?
!!
I DON'T WANT TO SEEM LIKE I'M PICKING ON YOU WEAKLINGS.
I'LL TAKE YOU ON WITH ONE FINGER.
CHING
PING
GAH!?

I'VE SOLD A BORING FIGHT.
THUD
ONE FLICK ...
A WHA... WHA...
PUNK.
SHK
THIS IS FINE AS A DRUNKEN BRAWL.
BUT IF YOU'RE GOING TO DRAW A CONCEALED BLADE...

DEMOCRATIC RIGHTS DESERVE SUPPORT.
......
BUT YOU NEED TO STRAIGHTEN *YOURSELVES* OUT BEFORE YOU STRAIGHTEN OUT THE GOVERNMENT.
PAY YOUR CHECK AND GO HOME.
THANK YOU SO MUCH FOR HELPING...
YAY
YAY
YAY
YAY
YAY
NOTHING TO THANK ME FOR. I DID THIS FOR MY OWN REASONS.
YAY
I APOLOGIZE FOR THE COMMOTION.
HEY, SWORDSMAN...
HOW'S THE WOUND ON YOUR HEAD?
TM
MM. NOT SO BAD, REALLY.
GOOD.
IT'D BE TOO BAD IF YOU GOT SERIOUSLY WOUNDED FROM GETTING HIT ON *PURPOSE*.
HUH?

IF YOU'D DODGED IT, THE LADY'S FACE WOULD BE ALL BLOODY RIGHT NOW.
SO YOU DIDN'T MOVE. YOU USED YOUR *HEAD* AS A *SHIELD*. AM I WRONG?
YOU GIVE ME TOO MUCH CREDIT.
HM
SUCH MODESTY.
PFT
I LIKE YOU. MIGHT YOU WANT TO BUY A FIGHT FROM ME?
GNG
I THINK IT WOULD BE A GOOD ONE.
THANK YOU, BUT NO.
WELL, IF YOU CHANGE YOUR MIND, BUY ONE FROM ME ANYTIME.
I'LL BE AT THE GOROTSUKI NAGAYA IN THE OUTSKIRTS OF THE CITY.
御服屋
TMF
LATER.
!

READ THIS WAY

悪
WHAT WAS THAT?
IS HE A GOOD GUY OR A BAD GUY?
OR JUST A WEIRD GUY...
HE WAS ODD...
WAIT--!
GASP
YOU KNOW HIM, TAE-SAN?
HE DIDN'T PAY HIS BILL...
...
KLUNK

READ THIS WAY

BUT HOW DID YOU FELLOWS MANAGE TO ESCAPE JAIL?
BY HATRED. PURE AND SIMPLE.
IT WOULD HAVE ALL GONE PERFECTLY IF HE HADN'T SHOWN UP ...
GRNG
RETALIATION. HOW PATHETIC.
MMG MMG
AND THIS KENSHIN-- HE'S REALLY GOOD?
I REFUSE TO FIGHT ANYONE WEAK. MY RECENT FIGHTS HAVE BEEN BORING, AND I'M GETTING TIRED OF IT.
HE'S INCREDIBLE! HE BEAT ME IN ONE BLOW!
SHF
FOOL!! KILLING YOU TEN THOUSAND TIMES WOULDN'T BE PROOF OF ANYTHING!
RRRG
PLEASE... JUST LISTEN TO ME.
HEY HEY. DON'T GET YOUR UGLY FACE NEAR MINE.
BOO HOO

READ THIS WAY
THIS KENSHIN IS...
.....!
IS THAT SO?
HOW IS THAT, ZANZA-SAN? WOULD HE BE A WORTHY OPPONENT?
YES.
WORTHY EVEN OF THIS, WHICH I HAVEN'T USED IN YEARS.
GG
THE LEGENDARY HITOKIRI... HIMURA BATTŌSAI!!
HYAH
THE FIGHT MERCHANT HAS BEEN LOOKING FOR A MAN LIKE YOU!!

The Secret Life of Characters (4)

—Hiruma Kihei & Gohei—

The way these two turned out is a direct function of the story. I wanted a pair of interesting villains to start things off with a bang, and figured I'd make one of them "brainy" and one of them "wild." The story of how these two first came together was taking up too many pages, though, so after some thought I made the decision to change them from being circumstantially related to being blood-related. Thus, they became brothers.

Models in terms of design are a certain well-known manager/director from Obata Takeshi's (sumō manga) *"Chikarabito Densetsu"* for Kihei... and some character spotted in a magazine who made me think, "Ooh, *impact!*" for Gohei. (Much more than that, I don't recall.)

Unlike Kenshin and the others, the faces of these two are made of basic, simple shapes, making them that much easier to draw. The closer I got to my deadlines, in fact, the fonder I became of them. Alas, we're not likely to see them again. (Heh.)

Time to draw them? About two minutes. Mm-m...easy!

READ THIS WAY

KAMIYA KAORU (17)
HIMURA KENSHIN (28)
MYŌJIN YAHIKO (10)
Act 6
Face Off: Sagara Sanosuke
SAGARA SANOSUKE (19)
HIRUMA GOHEI (37)
HIRUMA KIHEI (45)

FOOEY
WIG
"THE LEGENDARY HITOKIRI... HIMURA BATTŌSAI!!"
"THE FIGHT MERCHANT HAS BEEN LOOKING FOR A MAN LIKE YOU!!"
IT'S BEEN TWO WEEKS SINCE HE SAID THAT AND LEFT!
WHERE'D THAT BIRD HEAD GO?!
YAAAA!
BETTER NOT HAVE GOTTEN SCARED AND RAN AWAY.
MNCH
"I JUST NEED TO ENJOY MY FIGHT," HE SAYS.
WHAT AN IDIOT!!
GONN
REAL
YOU'RE THE IDIOT!!
!!!

READ THIS WAY

AKU=EVIL

READ THIS WAY

HENH
HE'S THE ONLY ONE WHO'LL BE ABLE TO KILL THAT ANNOYING MAN.
THAT HIMURA BATTŌSAI !!
PWIK
WE HAVE A GUEST...
KOP
HUH?
WAIT, KENSHIN ...
WHAT'S GOING ON?
SHP
SHP
HIS CHI IS POWERFUL.

UN-CONCEALED...
BLATANTLY HONEST FIGHTING CHI.
I CAME...
TO PICK A FIGHT.
THE GUY FROM BEFORE...!
SO IT'S YOU.
SORRY. THIS ONE SHALL REFRAIN FROM FIGHTING.
I CAN'T ACCEPT THAT.
I'VE TAKEN THIS FIGHT AS A MERCHANT. I CAN'T BACK OUT.
TP
ON TOP OF THAT...
...MY OPPONENT IS THE REVOLUTION-ARY WARRIOR HIMURA BATTŌSAI...

READ THIS WAY

!!
THE CHŌSHŪ REVOLUTIONARY, HIMURA BATTŌSAI...
WHOSE WAY IS THE ANCIENT SWORD-SCHOOL OF HITEN MITSURUGI-RYŪ...
...ACTIVE FOR FIVE YEARS, FROM AGES 14 TO 19...
...HIRED FOR THE FIRST HALF OF HIS CAREER...
...AS A HITOKIRI...
...A RELENTLESS ASSASSIN LURKING IN THE DARKNESS OF THE NIGHT...
...AND, IN THE LATTER HALF, ACTING AS A FREE SWORDSMAN TO PROTECT HIS COMRADES FROM THE GOVERNMENT'S KILLERS, THE SHINSENGUMI.
THUS THE KILLER WHO WOULD NEVER HAVE SEEN THE LIGHT OF DAY BECAME A LEGEND.
AND IN THE DECIDING BATTLE OF THE BOSHIN WAR...
...AFTER VICTORY IN THE FIRST BATTLE AT TOBA FUSHIMI, HE DISAPPEARS. AND REAPPEARS AS A RUROUNI. HIMURA KENSHIN.

READ THIS WAY
A REAL FIGHT BEGINS WITH KNOWING THE OPPONENT.
UPON LEARNING, I THEN CHOOSE THE WAY TO FIGHT.
I WENT TO KYOTO, WHERE THE REVOLUTION HAD ITS CENTER. I HAVE IT PRETTY MUCH RIGHT, DON'T I?
...AND HAVE YOU DETERMINED THE WAY TO FIGHT ME?
THAT'S THE PROBLEM!
MY RESEARCH ONLY TURNED UP A VAGUE HISTORY.
NOTHING ABOUT WHAT HITEN MITSURUGI-RYU IS LIKE...
...OR WHY THE RELENTLESS HITOKIRI TURNED INTO A RUROUNI WHO KILLS NO ONE.
SHH
SHH
I COULDN'T FIGURE IT OUT.
SO HERE I AM AT THE MAIN GATE, HONORABLY, ASKING FOR A FACE-TO-FACE FIGHT.
....

READ THIS WAY

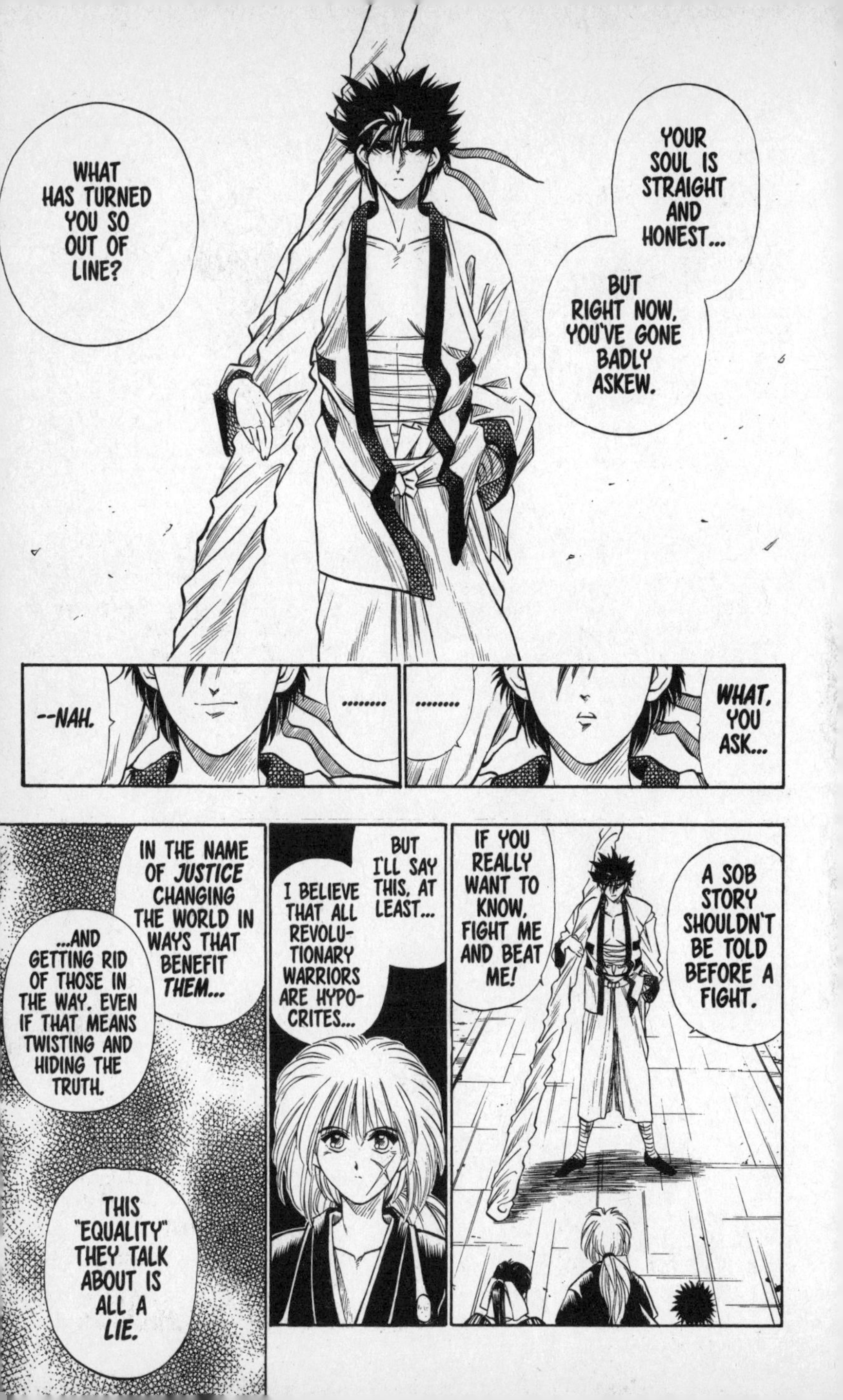

YOUR SOUL IS STRAIGHT AND HONEST...
BUT RIGHT NOW, YOU'VE GONE BADLY ASKEW.
WHAT HAS TURNED YOU SO OUT OF LINE?
WHAT, YOU ASK...
....
....
--NAH.
A SOB STORY SHOULDN'T BE TOLD BEFORE A FIGHT.
IF YOU REALLY WANT TO KNOW, FIGHT ME AND BEAT ME!
BUT I'LL SAY THIS, AT LEAST...
I BELIEVE THAT ALL REVOLUTIONARY WARRIORS ARE HYPOCRITES...
IN THE NAME OF *JUSTICE* CHANGING THE WORLD IN WAYS THAT BENEFIT *THEM*...
...AND GETTING RID OF THOSE IN THE WAY. EVEN IF THAT MEANS TWISTING AND HIDING THE TRUTH.
THIS "EQUALITY" THEY TALK ABOUT IS ALL A LIE.

I WANT TO CRUSH THE HITOKIRI WHOM THE SONGS CALL THE GREATEST OF THE REVOLUTIONARIES!!
GLLP
.....
KENSHIN!
ALL RIGHT, THEN.
BUT TELL ME THIS.
THE ONES WHO HIRED YOU ARE THE HIRUMA BROTHERS, YES?
EEP
YES. HOW DID YOU KNOW?
NOT MANY PEOPLE KNOW MY BACK-GROUND IN THIS CITY.
TP

READ THIS WAY
BESIDES... SOME VERY DIRTY CHI IS COMING IN FROM THAT SIDE OF THE FENCE.
SHOW YOUR-SELVES.
HEH. YOU'RE A GREAT WARRIOR, INDEED.
COME OUT, YOU TWO.
WE SAID, COME OUT.
....
BRRRR
ALL RIGHT, HAND IT OVER.
GOOD. GOOD. THERE YOU GO.
THUP
THUP
THUP
HS
HUH?
WHAT DO YOU MEAN, "HUH"?!
AH!

READ THIS WAY

Thanks for all the fan letters. For a new author, it's sure a lot of encouragement! A couple of you are mailing me every week, and 90% of you seem to be female––has "Shonen Jump" gone suddenly shōjo, I wonder? Anyway, these are the kinds of things I think of as I continue working on the series. I can't quite say I'll ever be able to reply to you, but I will always be sure to read each letter that comes my way. Thanks again for your support!

—Watsuki

伸宏和月

KINDA.
BUT IT'S FUNNY...
I DON'T FEEL AFRAID, KNOWING YOU WERE THE HITOKIRI BATTŌSAI.
IN FACT...
IT MAKES MORE SENSE TO ME NOW WHY YOU'RE AS GOOD AS YOU ARE.
ANYWAY, YOU THINK YOU'LL BE OKAY?
ORO?
I MEAN, LOOK AT HIS WEAPON. THAT'S GOT TO BE A SPEAR.
I HEARD YOU NEED THREE TIMES THE STRENGTH TO FIGHT A SPEAR WITH A SWORD.
THIS ISN'T A SPEAR, KID.
THIS IS...
...SOMETHING BETTER.

« READ THIS WAY «

SANOSUKE WITH THE SAN OR "ZAN" BATŌ.
ZANBATŌ...!
ZANBATŌ: A GIANT SWORD INVENTED BEFORE THE SENGOKU OR "WARRING STATES" PERIOD, DESIGNED TO TAKE DOWN A RIDER AND HIS HORSE IN ONE SWING.
IT IS THE HEAVIEST KATANA EVER MADE. BECAUSE OF ITS WEIGHT, IT IS SAID THAT NO ONE HAS EVER BEEN ABLE TO WIELD IT TO ITS FULL CAPACITY.
I'VE HEARD OF THIS...
ZANZA'S FAMOUS "PARTNER."
IT'S AN ANTIQUE FROM THE ŌNIN STRUGGLE, SO IT'S NOT IN PERFECT SHAPE ANYMORE...
GNNG
...SO EVEN THOUGH THEY CALL IT A *BLADE*, IT HAS NO EDGE AT ALL.
I CAN ONLY USE IT TO SMASH AND CRUSH.

ZANZA FOR SHORT.
HUMURA "RUROUNI" KENSHIN...
...WILL FACE YOU WITH THIS.
SHHHH
BUT THEN YOU PROBABLY ALREADY...
...KNEW THAT MUCH FROM YOUR RE-SEARCH.
YES. LET ME GIVE YOU SOME ADVICE.
LET GO OF YOUR IDEAS ABOUT SPARING LIVES.
...OR ELSE...

YOU'LL DIE!!!!
HE'S FAST!
WITH A WEAPON THAT HEAVY!
URAAAH!!

THUG!

READ THIS WAY

...OF COURSE. NO MATTER HOW BIG HIS ZANBATŌ IS, IT DOESN'T MATER IF HE CAN'T HIT!
IT'S AN EASY WIN FOR KENSHIN!
GNG
!
YOU ARE WORTHY OF YOUR LEGEND.
HSSSS
I'M GLAD.
NO... WAIT...
WE'VE BEEN MISREADING HIS STRENGTH...
HIS REAL STRENGTH ISN'T THE ZANBATŌ...
IT ISN'T EVEN THE MONSTROUS POWER THAT TAKES DOWN A GIANT MAN IN ONE FLICK.
HE DIDN'T FLINCH WHEN HE GOT HIT IN THE HEAD BY A SUNTETSU.
HIS STRENGTH IS HIS INHUMAN TOUGHNESS!!

TO BE CONTINUED IN VOLUME 2: THE TWO HITOKIRI!

READ THIS WAY

Rurouni Kenshin

Meiji Swordsman Romantic Story

The "side-story" you're about to read next was published about a year before the current series started. I remember what a hard time I had condensing everything down into 31 pages. This was my very first appearance in *Shonen Jump* magazine, and so of course I put all my soul into it, but when I look back now.... (Sigh.)

For me, the most memorable part was when Kenshin—his name wasn't mentioned yet, but Battōsai's "real" name was set a year before this saw print—changes his tone. My editor and I had very different opinions about this, right up to the very end, and ultimately we gave the character a more "slangy" speech pattern.

This time around, I tinkered a bit with his dialogue, making him sound more as I prefer him now, and still I think about what this story might have been if I'd had two more pages. Once it was finally published in *Jump,* I received mediocre reviews and about 200 letters, and although I was unable to reply to most of them, I'd like to take this opportunity now to thank you for your support then.

—Raikōji Chizuru—

This character is based on the "Chizuru" of Tomita Tsuneo's novel *"Sugata Sanshirō"* (whom else?). Upon the realization that there can be romance not only in saving someone who's being hurt, but in saving someone *before* they're hurt, I longed to write this particular story. Then again, Kaoru and Chizuru are so similar...long-lost sisters, perhaps? (Uh-oh. Guess it would *really* turn into the world of Sugata Sanshirō, then.) Chizuru is one of my favorite characters, and I'd love to bring her back, given the opportunity.

No motif in her design; I just wanted to draw a girl in *hakama.* I've done the sheltered rich girl, the kendō girl...will that make the next a priestess, eh, Watsuki?

END-OF-VOLUME SPECIAL (1)
RUROUNI
MEIJI SWORDSMAN ROMANTIC STORY

LONG AGO, IN KYOTO DURING THE REVOLUTION...
THERE LIVED A WARRIOR CALLED "HITOKIRI BATTŌSAI."
HE KILLED MEN LIKE AN OGRE...
...UNTIL HE DISAPPEARED WITH THE END OF THE REVOLUTION.
BUT TIME FLOWS ON, AND NOW...
IN THE 10TH YEAR OF MEIJI...
TMTMTM
STOP, DAMNIT!!
HEY! YOU THERE!
HUF
HUF

ORO?
WHAT INCREDIBLE TIMING!
ORO-RO?
WHADDA YOU MEAN "ORO"? A DAMSEL'S BEING CHASED! IF YOU'RE A MAN, HELP ME!
ORO?
WHO THE HELL ARE YOU?!
IF YOU DON'T WANT TO DIE, HAND OVER RAIKŌJI'S DAUGHTER!
SHP
TM
--WHAT?
A SWORD!
YOU'RE BREAKING THE LAW!
AND YOUR KNIVES ARE ANY BETTER?
YEAH
YEAH YEAH

SH
KILL HIM!!
YEAH, AND WE GOT TWO OF 'EM!!
HMM... NOT SUCH A PEACEFUL TOWN...
PAP
THERE'S NO CHOICE.
HUH?
GET BACK HERE!!
VRRRROOOM
YOU COWARD!!
PHEW.
SEEMS LIKE THEY DON'T WANT TO COME INTO THE CITY.
HOW LONG ARE YOU GONNA HOLD ME, PERVERT?!
BONK
ORO?
SORRY, SORRY. NO OFFENSE WAS MEANT.

YOU LOOK LIKE A SWORDSMAN, BUT YOU SURE DON'T ACT LIKE ONE.
YOU RAN LIKE A MOUSE.
IT'S BEST IF WE CAN AVOID FIGHTING, DON'T YOU THINK?
WHAT A WASTE. YOUR SWORD MUST BE CRYING.
MY SWORD DOESN'T MATTER.
IT CAN'T SLASH ANYTHING TO BEGIN WITH.
THIS ONE IS MERELY A *RUROUNI.*
HE DOESN'T MAKE A LIVING BY MY SWORD.
A WANDERING SAMURAI.
IN MEIJI?
I DIDN'T THINK THERE *WERE* ANY MORE SAMURAI, WANDERING OR...
RURO-UNI?
UNI
UNI
UNI=SEA URCHIN
ANYHOW, TAKE A LESSON FROM TODAY AND STOP MESSING WITH BOYS.
WHAAAA?!
GNG
GNG
HM? YOU MEAN THIS ISN'T ABOUT MISPLACED PASSIONS?
WHAT DO YOU TAKE ME FOR?
I DON'T EVEN KNOW WHO THEY *ARE!*
THEY'RE JUST PERVERTS WHO TRIED TO *KIDNAP* ME!

BUT THEY DID SEEM TO KNOW WHO YOU ARE...
EVERYONE AROUND HERE KNOWS I'M RAIKŌJI'S ONLY DAUGHTER.
ANYWAY, SINCE YOU SAVED ME, I'LL INVITE YOU TO THE HOUSE.
FWIP
FOLLOW ME!
THIS ONE WOULD HATE TO...
QUIT DRAGGING!
MMG!
HURRY UP!
Y...
YES, MA'AM...
TP TP TP
HERE.
IT'S APPARENT THAT YOU WERE DRESSED WELL... BUT THAT YOU SHOULD COME FROM *SUCH* WEALTH...
I'M JUST THE GRAND-DAUGHTER OF A BIG-TIME MERCHANT.
KCH
WHAT'S WITH YOU?
....
IF GRANDPA SPOTS US WE'LL BE IN SERIOUS TROUBLE, SO LET'S GO AROUND THE BACK DOOR.
TROUBLE ...SHE SAYS...

BECAUSE YOU LOOK LIKE A SWORDSMAN.
EVEN IF IT'S JUST DRESS-UP.
MHM
TP
CHIZURU.
EEEP
GRANDPA...
WHO IS THAT MAN?
UMM...HE'S KIND OF WEIRD, BUT HE'S HARMLESS.
HE SAVED ME FROM SOME KIDNAPPERS.
HELLO!
GET OUT!
NO ONE WHO CARRIES A SWORD CAN BE TRUSTED.
MAKE HASTE OUT OF THIS HOUSE.
I DIDN'T THINK IT WOULD WORK.
THIS ONE IS NOT VERY POPULAR.
DON'T LET IT BOTHER YOU, IT'S NOT JUST YOU.
HE HATES ALL SAMURAI AND SWORDSMEN.
ORO?

GRANDPA'S SON AND HIS WIFE...
MY PARENTS ...
WERE KILLED.
THEY GOT CAUGHT IN THE MIDDLE OF A BATTLE BETWEEN THE GOVERNMENT AND THE REVOLUTIONARY WARRIORS.
IT'S ALREADY BEEN TEN YEARS, BUT HE STILL HANGS ONTO IT...
I DON'T EVEN REMEMBER MY PARENTS' FACES.
THINK ABOUT IT. I WAS ONLY A BABY THEN.
SO I'M NOT SO SAD AT ALL.
HOW UN-FORTUNATE.
CRY ALL YOU WANT IN THIS ONE'S ARMS.
G
M
I'M NOT HANGING ONTO IT!
Ouch!

....
I KNOW. YOU THINK I'M COLD.
BUT I CAN'T HELP IT. WHAT I DON'T REMEMBER, I DON'T REMEMBER.
I CAN'T FEEL SAD...
EVEN IF I TRY.
COULD YOU GET SAD OVER A RELATIVE YOU DON'T KNOW?!
SHOULD I CRY BECAUSE MY COUSIN'S AUNT'S BROTHER-IN-LAW'S GREAT GRANDFATHER CROAKED?!
Easy... Eeeasy...
ZEE HUF ZEE HUF
FAN FAN
WHEW!
ANYHOW, I'M SORRY.
I INVITED YOU BUT IT DIDN'T GO SO WELL...
NO.
PLEASE DON'T APOLOGIZE.
ALL THIS ONE DID WAS RUN ANYWAY.
MAKING TOO BIG A DEAL ABOUT IT WILL ONLY MAKE THIS ONE FEEL WORSE.

READ THIS WAY
THAT SWORD REALLY DOES NOT SUIT YOU...
ALL RIGHT. BUT LET ME AT LEAST FEED YOU DINNER.
ORO?
WHERE ARE YOU STAYING? I'LL BRING YOU SOME FOOD LATER.
NO, PLEASE, IT'LL BE DARK SOON!
OH, DON'T BE SO HUMBLE.
YOU SHOULD ACCEPT PEOPLE'S KINDNESS MORE.
AND YOU SHOULD LISTEN TO PEOPLE MORE...
TEE HEE

THE REVOLUTIONARY WARRIORS—
SIGH
THEY GOT CAUGHT IN THE MIDDLE OF A BATTLE BETWEEN THE GOVERNMENT AND THE REVOLUTIONARY WARRIORS.
THEY WERE KILLED.
RUROUNI--
HMM... WHERE IS HE?
SAID HE DOESN'T HAVE ANY MONEY, SO HE'S SLEEPING UNDER THE BRIDGE...
TP
TP
THERE'S A LOT OF BRIDGES AROUND HERE...
TP
TP
RURO—
SHF

NK.
AH ...
FSH
I THOUGHT WE WERE FINISHED WHEN THAT JERK SHOWED UP.
...BUT WE'RE LUCKY.
TAKE THE HOSTAGE TO OUR LEADER!
I'LL GO THROW THE LETTER INTO THE RAIKŌJI MANSION.
SHE WAS HERE. SHE REALLY CAME.
TP
TP
BUT WHY DIDN'T SHE...

....
"RAIKŌJI MUNEIWA. THIS IS YOUR CRIME. YOU TRADE WITH THE EUROPEAN PIGS, ENRICHING YOURSELF AS YOU VIOLATE THIS LAND OF THE GODS, JAPAN.
"ALL WHO INHERIT YOUR BLOOD INHERIT YOUR GUILT. WE JUDGE YOUR GRAND-DAUGHTER GUILTY OF YOUR CRIMES.
"BUT WE ARE MISSIONARIES AND NOT OGRES. WE HAVE MERCY EVEN UPON THE WICKED.
"WITH AN OFFERING TO THE GODS OF 1000 YEN, WE WILL SAVE HER LIFE. YOU SHALL BRING THE MONEY TO THE ABANDONED TEMPLE ON YŪKYŪ MOUNTAIN BEFORE THE SUN RISES.
"IF YOU SCORN THE GODS, THIS YOUNG GIRL'S SOUL WILL PASS TO THE UNDERWORLD FOR ETERNITY. SHINSHŪ KONOE-BUSHIDAN KAITEN PARTY."
SOUNDS LIKE SOME FALLEN SAMURAI WHO AREN'T HAPPY ABOUT THE GOVERNMENT.
SHP
TNG
SAMURAI AGAIN!
TEN YEARS HAVE PASSED, AND STILL THOSE MONSTERS DO NOT THINK OF PEOPLE'S LIVES AS LIVES.
BAM

READ THIS WAY
I'M AN EX-SAMURAI MYSELF... SO LET'S PRETEND YOU DIDN'T SAY THAT.
WE'LL SEND A SCOUT, PREPARE A STRATEGY, AND REPORT BACK TO YOU.
WHAT?
I CAN'T WAIT FOR THAT!
I'M GOING THERE NOW!!
YOU'LL BE RISKING YOUR LIFE...!
I DON'T CARE! IF CHIZURU IS SAFE, LET ME DIE!!
NOW, NOW. YOU SHOULDN'T SAY THINGS LIKE THAT.
WAH
HMM. ABANDONED TEMPLE ON YŪKYŪ MOUNTAIN...
WOH
FFMP
!!
YOUR LOVELY GRANDCHILD WAS SPARED THE PAIN OF HER PARENTS' DEATH BECAUSE SHE WAS A BABY.
WHAT WILL HAPPEN IF SHE LOSES YOU NOW? SHE'LL BE IN TERRIBLE GRIEF...
WHEN DID YOU --?!!
JUST NOW.
GNNG
FROM WHERE?!
FRONT DOOR.
ANYWAY, WE CAN'T LET YOU DIE.

AND WHAT ABOUT YOU?
TM
THE SADNESS OF LOSING A LOVED ONE...
...NO ONE SHOULD SUFFER THAT TWICE.
HSH
...AND THIS TIME, ALONE.
CAN YOU LET HER SUFFER THAT?
STOP HIM, CAPTAIN! IF ANY-THING GOES WRONG—
VSH
HE'S GOING TO ATTACK THEM!
THAT MAN ...
GASP
YOUR PARDON.

HIS EYES ARE THOSE OF A DIFFERENT PERSON...
BUT THAT VOICE AND RED HAIR...
...AND THAT UNMISTAKABLE CROSS-SHAPED SCAR ON HIS LEFT CHEEK...
IT MUST BE HIM--!!
WELL, WELL. YOU AGAIN...
WHAT ARE YOU DOING HERE?!!
HOLD ON.
I DON'T THINK HE'S FROM THE GOVERNMENT.
PROBABLY SOME SWORDSMAN HIRED BY RAIKŌJI.
YOUNG MISS CHIZURU...
...HAD BETTER BE SAFE.

READ THIS WAY

ALIKE?
I DON'T THINK SO.
!!
RUROUNI...?
YOUR BANNERS ARE NOTHING BUT LIES.
AND HOW MANY OF YOU DOES IT TAKE TO CAPTURE ONE YOUNG GIRL?
TMP
YOUR ENVY IS OBVIOUS. THE ENVY OF THOSE WHO FAILED TO SEE THE FLOW OF TIME TOWARD THOSE WHO SAW IT.
YOU ...
RRR
...PUNK ...
KAITEN PARTY? WHAT A JOKE.
JUST CALL IT THE COWARD PARTY.
THK
KILL HIM!!!

YOU'LL WISH YOU'D LISTENED, FOOL!
H
VS
YOU'LL REGRET IT IN HELL!
!!
I WON'T HOLD BACK.
DO NOT BLAME ME FOR THIS.
HYU

HYAAA!
OH!

WH...
WH...
WHA... WHAT IS HE ?!!!
!!!

READ THIS WAY

READ THIS WAY

BUT ...
YOU CANNOT DEFEAT ME!!
EUROPEAN STEEL ARMOR...
YES. THE STRONGEST ARMOR IN THE WORLD.
NOT EVEN THE BEST SWORDS CAN PENE-TRATE...
TP
...THIS !!

NOW--
YOU DIE!!
TOO SLOW.

NICE DODGE!!
BUT YOU'LL NEVER SLASH THROUGH THIS--
NG!

OHH!!
DAMN IT...
WE'RE TOO LATE...
GUG... HAA...
TAKE A BETTER LOOK AT YOUR OPPONENT'S WEAPON BEFORE YOU BOAST ABOUT YOUR ARMOR.
PSH
PAK
PSH
PSH
A... SAKABATŌ ?!
NN!
THIS SWORD CAN'T CUT ANYTHING...

CAPTAIN, THEY'RE ALL ALIVE!
BROKEN BONES-- BUT NO FATAL WOUNDS!!
WHY...WOULD HITOKIRI BATTŌSAI...?
NO WAY...
JUST BEING A "HITOKIRI"...
KIN
DOESN'T MEAN THIS ONE *ENJOYS* KILLING PEOPLE.
....
ARE YOU ALL RIGHT, CHIZURU-DONO?
.....
SHWIP
OH, POOR GIRL. YOU'RE SO SCARED YOU CAN'T EVEN SPEAK...
GOOSH
DON'T GET CARRIED AWAY!
Ouch!

READ THIS WAY

GOOD.
GOOD.
THAT'S THE SPIRIT WE NEED IN THE AGE OF MEIJI.
BRING THAT ENERGY TO THE NEW WORLD WE'RE MAKING.
PFF
NOW ...
TP
TAKE CARE.
....
WAIT UP A MINUTE.
TM
TM
TM
TM
ZOOP
ORO ?

READ THIS WAY

LONG AGO, IN KYOTO DURING THE REVOLUTION...
THERE LIVED A WARRIOR CALLED "HITOKIRI BATTŌSAI."
HE KILLED MEN LIKE AN OGRE...
...UNTIL HE DIS-APPEARED WITH THE END OF THE REVOLU-TION.
BUT TIME FLOWS ON, AND IN THE 10TH YEAR OF MEIJI...
IN TOKYO --
HEE
HEE
A SWORDSMAN KNOWN AS "RUROUNI" ...
That man's wearing a ribbon.
It looks good, though.
HEE
HEE
ORO?
No clue that ribbons are for women.
...IS DRIFTING ALOOF WITHIN THE CURRENT OF TIME.
BUT IF THAT MAN WAS A WARRIOR IN THE REVOLUTION, HOW OLD IS HE NOW?
EVEN IF HE WERE YOUNG THEN, HE MUST BE PAST THIRTY.
EEP!
YOU'RE RIGHT!

RUROUNI • END

GLOSSARY of the RESTORATION

*A brief guide to select Japanese terms used in **Rurouni Kenshin**. Note that, both here and within the story itself, all names are Japanese style—i.e., last or "family" name first, with personal or "given" name following. This is both because **Kenshin** is a "period" story, as well as to decrease confusion—were we to reverse the order of the historically established assassin-name "Hitokiri Battôsai," for example, it would make little sense to then call him "Battôsai Himura."*

Hiten Mitsurugi-ryû
Kenshin's sword technique, used more for defense than offense. An "ancient style that pits one against many," it requires exceptional speed and agility to master

hitokiri
An assassin. Famous swordsmen of the period were sometimes thus known to adopt "professional" names—***Kawakami Gensai***, for example, was also known as "Hitokiri Gensai"

Ishin Shishi
Loyalist or pro-Imperialist ***patriots*** who fought to restore the Emperor to his ancient seat of power

Jigen-ryû
Aggressive swordsmanship style, characterized by one-handed draws/cuts, and the use of turning. Used in this story by Ujiki, a corrupt officer of the Police Sword Corps

Kamiya Kasshin-ryû
Sword-arts or ***kenjutsu*** school established by Kaoru's father, who rejected the ethics of ***Satsujin-ken*** for ***Katsujin-ken***

katsujin-ken
"Swords that give life"; the sword-arts style developed over ten years by Kaoru's father and founding principle of ***Kamiya Kasshin-ryû***

Kawakami Gensai
Real-life, historical inspiration for the character of ***Himura Kenshin***

kenjutsu
The art of fencing; sword arts; *kendô*

Kiheitai
Fighting force which included men of both the merchant and peasant classes

-kun

Aizu
Tokugawa-affiliated domain; fourth battle of the ***Boshin War***

Bakumatsu
Final, chaotic days of the Tokugawa regime

Boshin War
Civil war of 1868-69 between the new government and the ***Tokugawa Bakufu***. The anti-*Bakufu*, pro-Imperial side (the Imperial Army) won, easily defeating the Tokugawa supporters

-chan
Honorific. Can be used either as a diminutive (e.g., with a small child—"Little Hanako or Kentarô"), or with those who are grown, to indicate affection ("My dear...")

dojo
Martial arts training hall

-dono
Honorific. Even more respectful than ***–san***; the effect in modern-day Japanese conversation would be along the lines of "Milord So-and-So." As used by Kenshin, it indicates both respect and humility

Edo
Capital city of the ***Tokugawa Bakufu***, renamed ***Tokyo*** ("Eastern Capital") after the Meiji Restoration

Hijikata Toshizô
Vice-commander of the ***Shinsengumi***

Himura Battôsai
Swordsman of legendary skills and former assassin (*hitokiri*) of the ***Ishin Shishi***

Himura Kenshin
Kenshin's "real" name, revealed to Kaoru only at her urging

Honorific. Used in the modern day for male students, or those who grew up together, but another usage—the one you're more likely to find in **Rurouni Kenshin**—is the "superior-to-inferior" form, intended as a way to emphasize a difference in status or rank, as well as to indicate familiarity or affection

Kyoto
Home of the Emperor and imperial court from A.D. 794 until shortly after the Meiji Restoration in 1868

loyalists
Those who supported the return of the Emperor to power; ***Ishin Shishi***

Meiji Restoration
1853-1868; culminated in the collapse of the ***Tokugawa Bakufu*** and the restoration of imperial rule. So called after Emperor Meiji, whose chosen name was written with the characters for "culture and enlightenment"

patriots
Another term for ***Ishin Shishi***...and when used by Sano, not a flattering one

rurouni
Wanderer, vagabond

sakabatô
Reversed-edge sword (the dull edge on the side the sharp should be, and vice-versa); carried by Kenshin as a symbol of his resolution never to kill again

-san
Honorific. Carries the meaning of "Mr.," "Ms.," "Miss," etc., but used more extensively in Japanese than its English equivalent (note that even an enemy may be addressed as "*-san*")

satsujin-ken
"Swords that give death"; styles of swordsmanship rejected by Kaoru's father

Seinan War
1877 uprising of the samurai classes against the new Meiji government, ending in defeat by the government army. Also known as the "Satsuma Rebellion"

sensei
Teacher; master

Shinsengumi
Elite, notorious, government-sanctioned and exceptionally skilled swordsman-supporters of the military government (***Bakufu***) which had ruled Japan for nearly 250 years, the Shinsengumi ("newly selected corps") were established in 1863 to suppress the ***loyalists*** and restore law and order to the blood-soaked streets of the imperial capital (see ***Kyoto***)

shôgun
Feudal military ruler of Japan

shôgunate
See ***Tokugawa Bakufu***

suntetsu
Small, handheld blade, designed for palming and concealment

Tokugawa Bakufu
Military feudal government which dominated Japan from 1603 to 1867

Tokugawa Yoshinobu
15th and last ***shôgun*** of Japan. His peaceful abdication in 1867 marked the end of the ***Bakufu*** and beginning of ***Meiji***

Tokyo
The renaming of "***Edo***" to "***Tokyo***" is a marker of the start of the ***Meiji Restoration***

Toba Fushimi, Battle at
Battle near ***Kyoto*** between the forces of the new, imperial government and the fallen ***shôgunate***. Ending with an imperial victory, it was the first battle of the ***Boshin War***

Yamagata Aritomo
(1838-1922) Soldier and statesman, chief founder of the modern Japanese army. A samurai of Chôshû, he studied military science in Europe and returned to Japan in 1870 to head the war ministry

NARUTO
faces the most terrifying challenge of all:
EXAMS!
Only $7.95 Each
VOL.5 ON SALE DEC. 7TH!
VOL.1-4 ON SALE NOW!
SHONEN JUMP GRAPHIC NOVELS
NARUTO © 1999 by MASASHI KISHIMOTO / SHUEISHA Inc. COVER ART SUBEJCT TO CHANGE.

Ichigo's next opponent is...
his own mother?!
BLEACH
ブリーチ
Vol. 1-3
Available
Now!
on sale now at
www.shonenjump.com
Also available at your local
bookstore, comic store and
Suncoast Motion Picture Company.
COMIC SHOP LOCATOR SERVICE
888-COMIC-BOOK
888-266-4226
BLEACH © 2001 by TITE KUBO / SHUEISHA Inc.
COVER ART SUBJECT TO CHANGE.

SUBSCRIBE NOW!
12 ISSUES FOR ONLY $29.95
SHONEN JUMP
THE WORLD'S MOST POPULAR MANGA
FILL OUT THE SUBSCRIPTION CARD ON THE OTHER SIDE, OR SUBSCRIBE ONLINE AT:
www.shonenjump.com

Save 50% off the newsstand price!

SHONEN JUMP™

THE WORLD'S MOST POPULAR MANGA

Subscribe Now to the Magazine!

☑ **YES!** Please enter my one-year (12 issue) subscription to *SHONEN JUMP Magazine* at the **INCREDIBLY LOW SUBSCRIPTION RATE** of just **$29.95**

NAME

ADDRESS

CITY STATE ZIP

E-MAIL ADDRESS

☐ MY CHECK IS ENCLOSED ☐ BILL ME LATER

CREDIT CARD: ☐ VISA ☐ MASTERCARD

ACCOUNT # EXP. DATE

SIGNATURE

CLIP AND MAIL TO

SHONEN JUMP
Subscriptions Service Dept.
P.O. Box 515
Mount Morris, IL 61054-0515

Make checks payable to: **SHONEN JUMP.**
Canada add US $12. No foreign orders. Allow 6-8 weeks for delivery.

P309YG YU-GI-OH! © 1996 by KAZUKI TAKAHASHI / SHUEISHA Inc.

SHONEN JUMP
THE WORLD'S MOST POPULAR MANGA

COMPLETE OUR SURVEY AND LET US KNOW WHAT YOU THINK!

☐ Please do NOT send me information about VIZ and SHONEN JUMP products, news and events, special offers, or other information.

☐ Please do NOT send me information from VIZ's trusted business partners.

Name: ______________________________

Address: ______________________________

City: ____________ **State:** ________ **Zip:** ____________

E-mail: ______________________________

☐ **Male** ☐ **Female** **Date of Birth** (mm/dd/yyyy): ___/___/______ (**Under 13? Parental consent required**)

What race/ethnicity do you consider yourself? (please check one)

☐ Asian/Pacific Islander ☐ Black/African American ☐ Hispanic/Latino

☐ Native American/Alaskan Native ☐ White/Caucasian ☐ Other: ____________

What SHONEN JUMP Graphic Novel did you purchase? (indicate title purchased)

____

What other SHONEN JUMP Graphic Novels, if any, do you own? (indicate title(s) owned)

____

____

Reason for purchase: (check all that apply)

☐ Special offer ☐ Favorite title ☐ Gift

☐ Recommendation ☐ Read in SHONEN JUMP Magazine

☐ Read excerpt in the SHONEN JUMP Compilation Edition

☐ Other ______________________________

Where did you make your purchase? (please check one)

☐ Comic store ☐ Bookstore ☐ Mass/Grocery Store

☐ Newsstand ☐ Video/Video Game Store ☐ Other: ____________

☐ Online (site: ______________________________)

Do you read SHONEN JUMP Magazine?

- [ ] Yes
- [ ] No **(if no, skip the next two questions)**

Do you subscribe?

- [ ] Yes
- [ ] No

If you do not subscribe, how often do you purchase SHONEN JUMP Magazine?

- [ ] 1-3 issues a year
- [ ] 4-6 issues a year
- [ ] more than 7 issues a year

What genre of manga would you like to read as a SHONEN JUMP Graphic Novel?
(please check two)

- [ ] Adventure
- [ ] Comic Strip
- [ ] Science Fiction
- [ ] Fighting
- [ ] Horror
- [ ] Romance
- [ ] Fantasy
- [ ] Sports

Which do you prefer? (please check one)

- [ ] Reading right-to-left
- [ ] Reading left-to-right

Which do you prefer? (please check one)

- [ ] Sound effects in English
- [ ] Sound effects in Japanese with English captions
- [ ] Sound effects in Japanese only with a glossary at the back

THANK YOU! Please send the completed form to:

VIZ

VIZ Survey
42 Catharine St.
Poughkeepsie, NY 12601

All information provided will be used for internal purposes only. We promise not to sell or otherwise divulge your information.

NO PURCHASE NECESSARY. Requests not in compliance with all terms of this form will not be acknowledged or returned. All submissions are subject to verification and become the property of VIZ, LLC. Fraudulent submission, including use of multiple addresses or P.O. boxes to obtain additional VIZ information or offers may result in prosecution. VIZ reserves the right to withdraw or modify any terms of this form. Void where prohibited, taxed, or restricted by law. VIZ will not be liable for lost, misdirected, mutilated, illegible, incomplete or postage-due mail. © 2003 VIZ, LLC. All Rights Reserved. VIZ, LLC, property titles, characters, names and plots therein under license to VIZ, LLC. All Rights Reserved.